DATE DUE

GENERAL EDITORS

Dale C. Garell, M.D.
Medical Director, California Children Services, Department of Health
Services, County of Los Angeles
Clinical Professor, Department of Pediatrics & Family Medicine,
University of Southern California School of Medicine
Former president, Society for Adolescent Medicine

Solomon H. Snyder, M.D.
Distinguished Service Professor of Neuroscience, Pharmacology, and
Psychiatry, Johns Hopkins University School of Medicine
Former president, Society of Neuroscience
Albert Lasker Award in Medical Research, 1978

CONSULTING EDITORS

Robert W. Blum, M.D., Ph.D.
Associate Professor, School of Public Health and Department of
Pediatrics
Director, Adolescent Health Program, University of Minnesota
Consultant, World Health Organization

Charles E. Irwin, Jr., M.D.
Associate Professor of Pediatrics
Director, Division of Adolescent Medicine,
University of California, San Francisco

Lloyd J. Kolbe, Ph.D.
Chief, Office of School Health & Special Projects, Center for Health
Promotion & Education, Centers for Disease Control
President, American School Health Association

Jordan J. Popkin
Director, Division of Federal Employee Occupational Health, U.S. Public
Health Service Region I

Joseph L. Rauh, M.D.
Professor of Pediatrics and Medicine, Adolescent Medicine, Children's
Hospital Medical Center, Cincinnati
Former president, Society for Adolescent Medicine

THE ENCYCLOPEDIA OF
H E A L T H

PSYCHOLOGICAL DISORDERS
AND THEIR TREATMENT

Solomon H. Snyder, M.D. · General Editor

LEARNING
DISABILITIES

Jean McBee Knox

Introduction by C. Everett Koop, M.D., Sc.D.
Surgeon General, U.S. Public Health Service

CHELSEA HOUSE PUBLISHERS
New York · Philadelphia

The goal of the ENCYCLOPEDIA OF HEALTH *is to provide general information in the ever-changing areas of physiology, psychology, and related medical issues. The titles in this series are not intended to take the place of the professional advice of a physician or other health-care professional.*

53102

Chelsea House Publishers
EDITOR-IN-CHIEF Nancy Toff
EXECUTIVE EDITOR Remmel T. Nunn
MANAGING EDITOR Karyn Gullen Browne
COPY CHIEF Juliann Barbato
PICTURE EDITOR Adrian G. Allen
ART DIRECTOR Maria Epes
MANUFACTURING MANAGER Gerald Levine

The Encyclopedia of Health
SENIOR EDITOR Sam Tanenhaus

Staff for LEARNING DISABILITIES
ASSISTANT EDITOR Laura Dolce
COPY EDITOR Karen Hammonds
DEPUTY COPY CHIEF Nicole Bowen
EDITORIAL ASSISTANT Jennifer Trachtenberg
PICTURE RESEARCHER Debra P. Hershkowitz
ASSISTANT ART DIRECTOR Loraine Machlin
SENIOR DESIGNER Marjorie Zaum
PRODUCTION COORDINATOR Joseph Romano

90 -17389

3 5 7 9 8 6 4 2

Library of Congress Cataloging-in-Publication Data
Knox, Jean McBee.
Learning disabilities / Jean Knox;
introduction by C. Everett Koop.
p. cm.—(The Encyclopedia of health. Psychological
disorders and their treatment)
Bibliography: p.
Includes index.
Summary: Discusses the nature, possible causes, and treatment of
learning disabilities, how they are diagnosed, and whom they affect.
ISBN 0-7910-0049-4.
    0-7910-0529-1 (pbk.)
1. Learning disabilities—Juvenile literature. [1. Learning
disabilities.] I. Title. II. Series.   88-34174
RJ496.L4K59 1989   CIP
618.92'855—dc 19   AC

CONTENTS

THE ENCYCLOPEDIA OF

H E A L T H

PREVENTION AND EDUCATION: THE KEYS TO GOOD HEALTH

C. Everett Koop, M.D., Sc.D.
Surgeon General,
U.S. Public Health Service

The issue of health education has received particular attention in recent years because of the presence of AIDS in the news. But our response to this particular tragedy points up a number of broader issues that doctors, public health officials, educators, and the public face. In particular, it points up the necessity for sound health education for citizens of all ages.

Over the past 25 years this country has been able to bring about dramatic declines in the death rates for heart disease, stroke, accidents, and, for people under the age of 45, cancer. Today, Americans generally eat better and take better care of themselves than ever before. Thus, with the help of modern science and technology, they have a better chance of surviving serious—even catastrophic—illnesses. That's the good news.

But, like every phonograph record, there's a flip side, and one with special significance for young adults. According to a report issued in 1979 by Dr. Julius Richmond, my predecessor as Surgeon General, Americans aged 15 to 24 had a higher death rate in 1979 than they did 20 years earlier. The causes: violent death and injury, alcohol and drug abuse, unwanted pregnancies, and sexually transmitted diseases. Adolescents are particularly vulnerable, because they are beginning to explore their own sexuality and perhaps to experiment with drugs. The need for educating young people is critical, and the price of neglect is high.

Yet even for the population as a whole, our health is still far from what it could be. Why? A 1974 Canadian government report attributed all death and disease to four broad elements: inadequacies in the health-care system, behavioral factors or unhealthy life-styles, environmental hazards, and human biological factors.

To be sure, there are diseases that are still beyond the control of even our advanced medical knowledge and techniques. And despite yearnings that are as old as the human race itself, there is no "fountain of youth" to ward off aging and death. Still, there is a solution to many of the problems that undermine sound health. In a word, that solution is prevention. Prevention, which includes health promotion and education, saves lives, improves the quality of life, and, in the long run, saves money.

In the United States, organized public health activities and preventive medicine have a long history. Important milestones include the improvement of sanitary procedures and the development of pasteurized milk in the late 19th century, and the introduction in the mid-20th century of effective vaccines against polio, measles, German measles, mumps, and other once-rampant diseases. Internationally, organized public health efforts began on a wide-scale basis with the International Sanitary Conference of 1851, to which 12 nations sent representatives. The World Health Organization, founded in 1948, continues these efforts under the aegis of the United Nations, with particular emphasis on combatting communicable diseases and the training of health-care workers.

But despite these accomplishments, much remains to be done in the field of prevention. For too long, we have had a medical care system that is science- and technology-based, focused, essentially, on illness and mortality. It is now patently obvious that both the social and the economic costs of such a system are becoming insupportable.

Implementing prevention—and its corollaries, health education and promotion—is the job of several groups of people:

First, the medical and scientific professions need to continue basic scientific research, and here we are making considerable progress. But increased concern with prevention will also have a decided impact on how primary-care doctors practice medicine. With a shift to health-based rather than morbidity-based medicine, the role of the "new physician" will include a healthy dose of patient education.

Second, practitioners of the social and behavioral sciences—psychologists, economists, city planners—along with lawyers, business leaders, and government officials—must solve the practical and ethical dilemmas confronting us: poverty, crime, civil rights, literacy, education, employment, housing, sanitation, environmental protection, health care delivery systems, and so forth. All of these issues affect public health.

Third is the public at large. We'll consider that very important group in a moment.

Fourth, and the linchpin in this effort, is the public health profession—doctors, epidemiologists, teachers—who must harness the professional expertise of the first two groups and the common sense and cooperation of the third, the public. They must define the problems statistically and qualitatively and then help us set priorities for finding the solutions.

To a very large extent, improving those statistics is the responsibility of every individual. So let's consider more specifically what the role of the individual should be and why health education is so important to that role. First, and most obviously, individuals can protect themselves from illness and injury and thus minimize their need for professional medical care. They can eat a nutritious diet, get adequate exercise, avoid tobacco, alcohol, and drugs, and take prudent steps to avoid accidents. The proverbial "apple a day keeps the doctor away" is not so far from the truth, after all.

Second, individuals should actively participate in their own medical care. They should schedule regular medical and dental checkups. Should they develop an illness or injury, they should know when to treat themselves and when to seek professional help. To gain the maximum benefit from any medical treatment that they do require, individuals must become partners in that treatment. For instance, they should understand the effects and side effects of medications. I counsel young physicians that there is no such thing as too much information when talking with patients. But the corollary is the patient must know enough about the nuts and bolts of the healing process to understand what the doctor is telling him. That is at least partially the patient's responsibility.

Education is equally necessary for us to understand the ethical and public policy issues in health care today. Sometimes individuals will encounter these issues in making decisions about their own treatment or that of family members. Other citizens may encounter them as jurors in medical malpractice cases. But we all become involved, indirectly, when we elect our public officials, from school board members to the president. Should surrogate parenting be legal? To what extent is drug testing desirable, legal, or necessary? Should there be public funding for family planning, hospitals, various types of medical research, and medical care for the indigent? How should we allocate scant technological resources, such as kidney dialysis and organ transplants? What is the proper role of government in protecting the rights of patients?

What are the broad goals of public health in the United States today? In 1980, the Public Health Service issued a report aptly entitled *Promoting Health-Preventing Disease: Objectives for the Nation.* This report expressed its goals in terms of mortality and in terms of intermediate goals in education and health improvement. It identified 15 major concerns: controlling high blood pressure; improving family planning; improving pregnancy care and infant health; increasing the rate of immunization; controlling sexually transmitted diseases; controlling the presence of toxic agents and radiation in the environment; improving occupational safety and health; preventing accidents; promoting water fluoridation and dental health; controlling infectious diseases; decreasing smoking; decreasing alcohol and drug abuse; improving nutrition; promoting physical fitness and exercise; and controlling stress and violent behavior.

For healthy adolescents and young adults (ages 15 to 24), the specific goal was a 20% reduction in deaths, with a special focus on motor vehicle injuries and alcohol and drug abuse. For adults (ages 25 to 64), the aim was 25% fewer deaths, with a concentration on heart attacks, strokes, and cancers.

Smoking is perhaps the best example of how individual behavior can have a direct impact on health. Today cigarette smoking is recognized as the most important single preventable cause of death in our society. It is responsible for more cancers and more cancer deaths than any other known agent; is a prime risk factor for heart and blood vessel disease, chronic bronchitis, and emphysema; and is a frequent cause of complications in pregnancies and of babies born prematurely, underweight, or with potentially fatal respiratory and cardiovascular problems.

Since the release of the Surgeon General's first report on smoking in 1964, the proportion of adult smokers has declined substantially, from 43% in 1965 to 30.5% in 1985. Since 1965, 37 million people have quit smoking. Although there is still much work to be done if we are to become a "smoke-free society," it is heartening to note that public health and public education efforts—such as warnings on cigarette packages and bans on broadcast advertising—have already had significant effects.

In 1835, Alexis de Tocqueville, a French visitor to America, wrote, "In America the passion for physical well-being is general." Today, as then, health and fitness are front-page items. But with the greater scientific and technological resources now available to us, we are in a far stronger position to make good health care available to everyone. And with the greater technological threats to us as we approach the 21st century, the need to do so is more urgent than ever before. Comprehensive information about basic biology, preventive medicine, medical and surgical treatments, and related ethical and public policy issues can help you arm yourself with the knowledge you need to be healthy throughout your life.

FOREWORD

Solomon H. Snyder, M.D.

Mental disorders represent the number one health problem for the United States and probably for the entire human population. Some studies estimate that approximately one-third of all Americans suffer from some sort of emotional disturbance. Depression of varying severity will affect as many as 20 percent of all of us at one time or another in our lives. Severe anxiety is even more common.

Adolescence is a time of particular susceptibility to emotional problems. Teenagers are undergoing significant changes in their brain as well as their physical structure. The hormones that alter the organs of reproduction during puberty also influence the way we think and feel. At a purely psychological level, adolescents must cope with major upheavals in their lives. After years of not noticing the opposite sex, they find themselves romantically attracted but must painfully learn the skills of social interchange both for superficial, flirtatious relationships and for genuine intimacy. Teenagers must develop new ways of relating to their parents. Adolescents strive for independence. Yet, our society is structured in such a way that teenagers must remain dependent on their parents for many more years. During adolescence, young men and women examine their own intellectual bents and begin to plan the type of higher education and vocation they believe they will find most fulfilling.

Because of all these challenges, teenagers are more emotionally volatile than adults. Passages from extreme exuberance to dejection are common. The emotional distress of completely normal adolescence can be so severe that the same disability in an adult would be labeled as major mental illness. Although most teenagers somehow muddle through and emerge unscathed, a number of problems are more frequent among adolescents than among adults. Many psychological aberrations reflect severe disturbances, although these are sometimes not regarded as "psychiatric." Eating disorders, to which young adults are especially vulnerable, are an example. An extremely large number of teenagers diet to great excess even though they are not overweight. Many of them suffer from a specific disturbance referred to as anorexia nervosa, a form of self-starvation that is just as real a disorder as diabetes. The same is true for those who eat compulsively and then sometimes force themselves to vomit. They may be afflicted with bulimia.

Depression is also surprisingly frequent among adolescents, although its symptoms may be less obvious in young people than they are in adults. And, because suicide occurs most frequently in those suffering from depression, we must be on the lookout for subtle hints of despondency in those close to us. This is especially urgent because teenage suicide is a rapidly worsening national problem.

The volumes on Psychological Disorders and Their Treatment in the ENCYCLOPEDIA OF HEALTH cover the major areas of mental illness, from mild to severe. They also emphasize the means available for getting help. *Anxiety and Phobias, Depression*, and *Schizophrenia* deal specifically with these forms of mental disturbance. *Child Abuse* and *Delinquency and Criminal Behavior* explore abnormalities of behavior that may stem from environmental and social influences as much as from biological or psychological illness. *Personality Disorders* and *Compulsive Behavior* explain how people develop disturbances of their overall personality. *Learning Disabilities* investigates disturbances of the mind that may reflect neurological derangements as much as psychological abnormalities. *Mental Retardation* explains the various causes of this many-sided handicap, including the genetic component, complications during pregnancy, and traumas during birth. *Suicide* discusses the epidemiology of this tragic phenomenon and outlines the assistance available to those who are at risk. *Stress Management* locates the sources of stress in contemporary society and considers formal strategies for coping with it. Finally, *Diagnosing and Treating Mental Illness* explains to the reader how professionals sift through various signs and symptoms to define the exact nature of the various mental disorders and fully describes the most effective means of alleviating them.

Fortunately, when it comes to psychological disorders, knowing the facts is a giant step toward solving the problems.

LEARNING DISABILITIES

Imagine for a moment being inside a first-grade classroom. A six year old is reading aloud, slowly sounding out an unfamiliar word. Consider the number of skills this task involves. The boy's brain must make complex connections that enable him to recognize the 26 letters of the alphabet and their phonetic sounds. He must screen out all distractions—the fidgeting of the child in the seat behind him, the noises rumbling in the hallway—and focus all his attention on the page and its printed words, however tedious they may be. Given the magnitude of the task, it seems remarkable that this child and so many other children will manage to crack the code of written language.

Sometimes, however, a child does not master the skill of reading at age 6 as expected. Or at 7 or 10 or even 12 or 15. When this occurs, both the child and his or her parents may feel they have failed. Reading problems may not be the only reason for their sense of failure. Perhaps the child cannot sit still in a classroom, or simple addition and subtraction seem overwhelming. Directions may be hard to follow. The child may be clumsier than most and socially awkward. Somehow traditional teaching methods do not work. For whatever reasons, an otherwise intelligent, healthy child or adolescent sometimes feels out of step in school. Very often the child will begin to hear his or her problems referred to as "learning disabilities."

The term *learning disabilities* (LD) refers not to a single disorder but to a wide range of problems, most of which impair reading skills and, sometimes, writing skills, though some people with learning disabilities have trouble listening, speaking, reasoning, or doing math. Some learning-disabled people also have psychological problems or are slow to develop motor skills, and many have more than one disability. Because there is such a variety of learning disabilities and because they occur in so many combinations, each case seems unique.

The Learning-Disabled Student

Although there is a wide variety of learning disabilities, they constitute a distinct type of ailment and should not be confused with handicaps such as blindness, deafness, or mental retardation. Learning-disabled students are of at least average intelligence; many are extremely bright and excel in particular areas. Indeed, learning-disabled students often score high in puzzle and problem solving on intelligence tests, though they may earn poor marks for verbal expression (spoken or written words).

For most learning-disabled students, school is very difficult. Because society places great emphasis on doing well in school, many learning-disabled students often consider themselves stupid—a judgment often reinforced by the cruel taunting of their peers. Unfortunately, the fact that a learning disability is a "hidden handicap" does not always help those who suffer from it. If

A young girl takes a test designed to detect the presence of a learning disability.

they fail to perceive the problem, teachers may accuse the student of being lazy or unmotivated, unwilling to try when, in fact, he is trying his best. For this reason, many learning-disabled students hide their problem as long as possible—sometimes up to their high-school years—for fear of being treated differently or scorned. Others are simply too shy to ask for help. In fact, a student who suspects him- or herself of having a learning disability should tell his or her parents or teacher immediately. Like any other ailment, a learning disability can be treated only after it has been diagnosed. And treatment can help the student regain self-esteem through a better understanding of his or her disability.

Understanding Learning Disabilities

Some scientists estimate that as much as 40% of the world's population may have some form of learning disability. It is thus all the more disappointing that so few people truly understand what learning disabilities are and how they should be treated. All too often, learning-disabled people exist in an agony of fear and confusion, with few people understanding their problem. This volume discusses what learning disabilites are, when they were first recognized, and how a student can tell if he or she is learning disabled. We will discuss the varying degrees of disabilities and the different programs available to treat them, and see how students have overcome their learning disability and learned to cope.

•   •   •   •

CHAPTER 1

· · · · · · · · · · · · · · · · · ·

THE HISTORY
OF LEARNING
DISABILITIES

Dr. Samuel T. Orton.

The field of learning disabilities is a relatively new one. Indeed, most learning disorders went relatively unnoticed or misunderstood until the early part of the 20th century. At that time, James Hinshelwood, an eye doctor in Glasgow, Scotland, proposed the theory that a brain defect caused otherwise intelligent people to have extreme difficulty reading. Hinshelwood coined the term "congenital word-blindness" to describe this condition.

Hinshelwood's theories persisted until the 1920s, when neurologist Samuel T. Orton also began to speculate that some neurological "dysfunction" might cause reading disabilities. During World War II, neuroscientists treating soldiers whose brains had been injured in combat pursued Hinshelwood's theory by conducting the first studies that supported the theory that learning problems were related to a malfunction in the brain. These neuroscientists compared the learning deficits experienced by these injured soldiers with those of children who had reading difficulties. Still, it was not until the late 1960s that learning disabilities were generally recognized as a separate field of scientific study.

Unfortunately, scientists were unable to prove that a definite connection existed between learning problems and the brain. They were just beginning to realize, however, that the brain was a fascinating and promising area of research—one that possibly contained answers to any number of disorders, learning disabilities among them. Inspired by the efforts of parent organizations, and encouraged by improved medical technology, research on learning disabilities did not slide back into obscurity as it had in the past. Active organizations lobbied for more public attention and school funding for children with learning problems, as did parents' magazines and the press. Gradually, more and more children began to be diagnosed as learning disabled.

In 1973, Federal Law 94–142 recognized learning disabilities as an educational handicap and mandated that every public school system in the United States provide special education appropriate to the needs of learning-disabled students. From that point on, the learning-disabilities field developed rapidly because it gave a name to a common preexisting problem. Teachers had always had a few students for whom traditional educational methods did not work, but they had been unable to identify the problem; consequently, these children did not receive the care and attention they needed to flourish in school.

Similarly, many parents had known that their hyperactive or slow-to-read youngsters were not stupid. The acknowledgment of learning disabilities as disorders that are often only mildly disturbing (the sufferer can usually function normally in everyday life) confirmed their beliefs. Likewise, many adults learned with relief that their lifelong spelling problems, while perhaps

The inventor Thomas Edison is one of many well-known persons believed to have been learning disabled.

still embarrassing, had a real cause and also a name: *dyslexia*.

In light of the new evidence concerning learning disorders, historians and educators even began to theorize that many famous people had been learning disabled as children. Thomas Edison's spelling and grammar were atrocious. Albert Einstein was slow to talk and to read. President Woodrow Wilson, English prime minister Winston Churchill, and New York governor Nelson Rockefeller all were poor students. Artists Leonardo da Vinci and Auguste Rodin and authors Walt Whitman, William Butler Yeats, Hans Christian Andersen, and Agatha Christie all apparently had learning difficulties as well. And although it is possible that some of these creative people were simply too restless and inquisitive to excel in conventional classrooms, it is also likely that some of them suffered from learning disabilities.

In any case, much remains to be explained and discovered about learning disabilities. Much of what we take as fact is speculative, based on years of study and research but still incomplete and awaiting the clues that only a total understanding of the mysteries of the brain can uncover. There is some uncertainty among researchers about how best to diagnose learning problems. Doctors and educators do not always agree about which tests are most accurate. And symptoms of learning problems are not always easy to recognize; some can be mistaken for normal developmental problems.

The exact causes of learning disabilities remain unknown, although considerable evidence points to neurological differences (variations in arrangements of brain cells) in the brain. Scientists can now identify the areas within the brain's left hemisphere that control language development, which could prove to be a major breakthrough in determining the cause of many disorders. On the other hand, external factors such as tension at home and in school must also be taken into consideration.

Another issue about which many scientists disagree is the treatment of learning disabilities. For certain attention or hyperactive disorders, drugs can be effective, but they raise new questions. What is the correct dosage? What are the potential side effects? How long should drug treatment continue? Can other treatments—such as enrolling the student in a different school or trying out a different teaching method—bring about improvement? These questions lead to others. Should learning-disabled students be subjected to the same graduation requirements as other students? Where does a school's responsibility to its students end? Is special education better than "mainstreaming" (placement of an LD student in a regular classroom with students who do not have LDs), that is, keeping disabled students in classrooms with their "normal" peers? If special education or tutoring is better, who should pay for it—the government, the community, the student's family? All of these questions are confusing territory for parents, teachers, and young people.

There are some points of agreement on learning disability, however. For one thing, it is estimated that 20% of American schoolchildren have been designated learning-disabled. That translates into about 1.8 million cases, or an enormous 127% increase since 1976. The reason for this increase is not an epidemic of learning disorders but, rather, an increased awareness on the part of parents and educators of the symptoms of learning disabilities. Teachers are more attuned to learning disabilities than in times past and thus more apt to identify learning problems among their students. And parents are less resistant to having their child or adolescent tested for learning disabilities, especially because a learning-disability diagnosis qualifies a student for extra help.

Undoubtedly, some students assigned to learning-disabilities programs do not really belong there. They may have behavior problems or simply need some extra tutoring. Federal Law 94–142 (1973) emphasizes that a child suffering from a specific learning disability must receive an individualized educational program, but in many school districts funds are scarce. In such districts a child can receive the extra attention he or she may need only at a federally funded "learning skills room."

Today, much more is understood about learning disabilities than 20 years ago. This is because neuroscientists now have better tools for examining the brain and a better understanding of memory and learning. In addition, many learning-disabled students speak openly about their handicap, recover their self-esteem, and

Since 1976 there has been a 127% increase in the designation of children as learning disabled. This escalation is largely due to greater awareness by both teachers and parents.

learn to cope. Teachers often attend special seminars on learning disabilities, and at some elementary schools, kindergarten children who show evidence of having such disabilities receive extra help that enables them to move into the regular first-grade classroom. And colleges throughout the country are establishing special programs for learning-disabled students.

The learning disabled have something to teach everyone about how we learn. It is easy to take it for granted that a class of six- and seven-year-old children will learn to read. But the failures and achievements of the learning-disabled suggest that learning to read and write, to compute numbers, to concentrate, to follow directions, and generally to feel competent in school are precious, often hard won, and sometimes miraculous accomplishments.

•   •   •   •

CHAPTER 2

· · · · · · · · · · · · · · · · ·

WHAT ARE LEARNING DISABILITIES?

Just as there are dozens of terms and definitions for learning disabilities, there are also many symptoms of them. To add to the confusion, the terminology used to describe these problems is constantly changing as certain terms are deemed misleading or inadequate. For example, many learning disabilities used to be lumped under a condition called minimal brain dysfunction (MBD), which associated a variety of impairments, involving language, memory, attention, and motor control, with defects in various areas of the brain. But the old MBD term was too vague, describing only the suspected cause and not the nature of the problem. Today's official, all-encompassing term of learning disabilities is considered by some to be equally vague.

Learning disabilities are now divided into specific categories, each of which includes a wide range of disabilities, from mild and barely detectable learning problems to severe handicaps that require constant attention. Each individual's learning problems are apt to be found in a combination of overlapping categories. For example, a student may have an attention deficit hyperactive disorder (ADHD) without being hyperactive, mild dyslexia involving visual word memory, and poor hand-eye coordination.

In addition, some learning problems are not lifelong disabilities but developmental delays that may disappear, lessen, or become less obvious as a child gets older. It is important to note also that learning skills develop at different times in different children. Parents may become unnecessarily anxious if their second-grader cannot yet read, but these parents must understand that the reading development of that child may be delayed; that is, the child may not be ready to read until, for example, third grade. Parents may be equally anxious if their baby is slow to crawl, walk, or talk. Years later, when that baby has grown into a teenager and spends hours on the telephone or decides to take up rock climbing, they may laugh at their concern.

DYSLEXIA

Dyslexia is the term used to describe learning disorders involving written or spoken language. It is characterized by extreme difficulty learning and remembering letters, written or spoken words, and individual letter sounds. Bizarre spelling and illegible handwriting are common symptoms. Dyslexics sometimes reverse letters and words (*b* for *d*, *saw* for *was*) long past the age when most children have corrected this normal developmental tendency. In speech, some dyslexics reverse meanings (hot for cold, front seat for backseat) or word sounds (*merove* for *remove*).

Fortunately, most dyslexics suffer from only a few of these various problems. For example, they may be able to recognize individual letters but seem "word-blind." They may have weak

(continued on page 26)

Do You Have a Learning Disability?

Do you wonder if you have a learning disability? If you have reached high school without the assistance of special education classes or tutorial help, the chances are good that any problem you might have is a mild one. Most of the reasons for academic problems in high school are not related to learning disabilities. Poor study habits, heavy academic loads, difficult subject matter, too many extracurricular activities, and personal and family stress are more often to blame. On the other hand, if you are having serious academic difficulty no matter how hard you study, you may have an undiagnosed disability.

The most frequently displayed symptoms of learning disabilities are listed herein. Most of us exhibit a few of these characteristics at one time or another. But the persistence of a cluster of these problems could signify a learning disability.

- Short attention span, easily distracted.
- Restless hyperactivity.
- Poor letter or word memory.
- Poor auditory memory.
- Inability to discriminate between letters, numbers, or sounds.
- Poor handwriting.
- Reads poorly, if at all.
- Cannot follow multiple directions.
- Erratic performance from day to day.
- Impulsive.
- Poor coordination.
- Late gross or fine motor development.
- Difficulty telling time or distinguishing left from right.
- Late speech development, immature speech.
- Trouble understanding words or concepts.
- Trouble naming familiar people or things.
- Says one thing, means another.
- Responds inappropriately in many instances.
- Adjusts poorly to change.

The foregoing was reprinted from the Association for Children and Adults with Learning Disabilities (ACLD).

(continued from page 24)
auditory perception and be unable to distinguish between different vowel or consonant sounds. In some instances, their visual perception may be poor, making it hard to recognize individual letters or words in a sentence. Many dyslexics comprehend stories well and acquire a good spoken vocabulary but cannot write clearly.

Nearly two-thirds of all students with verbal disabilities suffer from educational, psychological, and cultural disadvantages that can be overcome. The remaining third are spatial dyslexics who cannot distinguish the spatial relationships of letters within words. For example, letters blur together, or the word *beat* is not easy to distinguish from *bet*, or *dog* looks much like *bog*. Therefore, one dyslexic may have persistent spelling problems that respond well to rigorous tutoring, whereas another may be hampered by a seemingly insurmountable reading handicap. Yet both may be diagnosed as dyslexic.

Dyslexia has been described as a catchall term that covers a constellation of language and speech problems found in about 5%–10% of all school-age children. Yet dyslexia differs so much from one individual to another that some neuroscientists suggest there is no single disorder called dyslexia and, further, that so

A student completes a language arts exercise. The objective of the lesson is to help the student identify and differentiate visually confusing letters such as b and d by picking them out of a manuscript passage.

many different conditions most likely have different causes. One consistent fact is that 80% of dyslexics are male. Scientists and educators believe the answer to this mystery can be found in the chromosomes. They believe it is possible that dyslexia is caused by a defect on chromosome 15—although it is also possible it stems from beginning school too early. Researchers also speculate that the condition may be inherited because dyslexia often runs in families.

Dyslexia is probably the best-known learning disability. Because of reading's overwhelming importance in school, dyslexia has received more attention than other learning disabilities. But "pure" cases of dyslexia, unaccompanied by other problems, are actually quite uncommon.

DYSCALCULIA

The term *dyscalculia* applies to difficulties some people have recognizing numbers and understanding basic mathematical concepts. It is less common than dyslexia but often appears in people with reading problems. Someone who has dyscalculia may fail to remember more than one number at a time, struggle to write legible numbers, and if he or she writes a column of numbers, it may drift to the left or the right of the page. Problems also occur on the level of logic and mathematical operations. A student may be consistently stumped by a straightforward math problem because he or she misunderstands the concept involved, uses an inappropriate procedure, or has trouble planning the correct steps. Difficulties may arise for the student when the information is presented with words rather than numbers or when the problem can be solved only by writing it on paper. Dyscalculia sufferers often simply guess at answers or use impulsive reasoning to mask their difficulty.

As an example of dyscalculia, consider the following word problem from *Learning Disabilities*, by Sylvia Farnham-Diggory: "A boy is eight years old. His father is thirty years older, and his mother is ten years younger than the father. How old are they?" Unable to understand the logic of the problem, a woman with dyscalculia gave this answer: "Each part here must have thirty and then ten and then eight, that makes forty-eight and divide by three." It took four tries before she solved the problem.

Students suffering from dyscalculia have difficulty with math—often they are unable to solve even the simplest arithmetic problems.

A person with dyscalculia might line up an addition problem in this way:

$$63$$
$$\underline{+\,2}$$

Not all the signs of dyscalculia are apt to show up at once. Simple calculations may be easy, whereas word problems involving numbers remain baffling. A student able to understand geometry problems and theorems may find the abstract concepts of algebra impossible. Some cases suggest a major disorder; in others, the person may respond to simple, if unorthodox, solutions. One student found that changing the word *plus* to the word *altogether* in an addition problem made all the difference in finding the solution.

Dyscalculia is different from "math anxiety," which is primarily a psychological problem. People with math anxiety know basic math but associate it with overwhelming stress and failure and thus have intense difficulty working at it. When relaxed and confident, their math problems usually disappear. People with dyscalculia also experience stress and failure, which makes it even harder for them to overcome the disability.

(continued on page 30)

Profile #1: "My Problems Began in High School"

Pete, 17, is from Croton, New York. He is tall, with sandy hair, and he speaks slowly, searching carefully for the right words to express himself. He is a student at a four-year liberal arts college.

"My problems began in high school. Grade school wasn't very hard, but in high school there was this whole wall of information coming at me and I couldn't handle it. They just said I was a borderline student and didn't do anything about it.

"When I was a freshman in high school, we moved to another town. I didn't want to move, even though I wasn't doing too well at my old school either. It was hard to fit in at the new school—there were all sorts of cliques. Because I had moved and wasn't doing so well, I got kind of depressed. I had good teachers; that wasn't the problem.

"Then my senior year they gave me these tests like the Wechsler. There were two parts to the test. On the memory part I got them all right, but I did real bad on the others. They said it was not a big disability—it might have just been anxiety about the test. But I was kind of mad that they didn't tell me about it or give me any help until my senior year.

"The things I'm not interested in fly out of my head. But it's funny, when I do learn something it sticks in my head forever. I remember stuff other people forget.

"My writing and spelling are bad. When I have to take notes in class, the teacher goes too fast. The structure is hard for me, like I can't figure out where to put a semicolon. And reading's hard—I don't read very fast. Reading with tapes is so much easier. I can understand the tape. It's strange, but if I'm hearing something, I'm into it.

"Anyone who wonders if they have a learning disability should step forward and say: 'Maybe you should give me a test.' Because in my experience, no one is going to ask you if you're all right. And I hate to say it, but asking for help is very hard to do.

"You have to have a sense of humor. Once in a while here someone will ask: 'So what's your LD?' Sometimes kids here talk about how hard it is—but they also laugh about it."

(continued from page 28)

ATTENTION DEFICIT HYPERACTIVE DISORDER

The term *attention deficit hyperactive disorder* (ADHD) is applied to attention problems. One of the many disorders that educators and scientists once called minimal brain dysfunction, ADHD inhibits those afflicted with it from focusing on a single task, concentrating for an extended period of time, or screening out distracting information. A person with ADHD often cannot finish a project and may not appear to be listening or may interrupt frequently. It may be difficult for the student to sit still in class. Often, he or she will act impulsively, wandering around the classroom or banging on a desk. He or she may also have a hot temper that leads to aggressive behavior. According to the American Psychiatric Association, ADHD has as many as 14 different symptoms. For a diagnosis to be made, a child must exhibit at least eight of these symptoms.

Like dyslexia, ADHD is probably not just one disability but several, with different causes requiring different treatments. About one-third to two-thirds of those who have ADHD as children continue to have it into adulthood. Estimates of the number of American schoolchildren with ADHD vary widely, from as low as 3% to as high as 15%. The disorder afflicts six to nine times more boys than girls.

Hyperactivity is not a clear-cut syndrome, but it is different from simple childhood exuberance. A hyperactive child cannot willingly control his or her "wild" behavior and may fluctuate from moments of quiet and industriousness to moments when he or she is noisy and disruptive. In addition to attention problems, the hyperactive child has unusual energy and restlessness and often touches, pokes, pushes, and fights.

Hyperactivity was once the standard diagnosis for children with ADHD. Hyperactive children usually had the most obvious attention problems and caused the most chaos for teachers. But the hyperactivity diagnosis omitted many other cases of ADHD. Researchers now understand more about various kinds of attention. There is *caught* attention, when something interrupts our thoughts or "catches" our eye. There is *focused* attention, which involves a deliberate choice to concentrate on one set of instruc-

For children suffering from a spatial deficit a moving ball may seem closer than it really is, and first base may appear to be very far away.

tions or one task. There is *sustained* attention, which is necessary for finishing a project, understanding a complicated list of instructions, or listening to a long story. And there is *selective* attention, which allows us to screen out anything that interferes with the task at hand. ADHD may interfere with any one or several of these aspects of attention.

In fact, because every aspect of learning requires attention, some researchers suspect that ADHD is the root cause of most learning disorders. For example, a dyslexic child may not hear a short-vowel sound in a word because he or she cannot focus attention long enough to hear it or cannot concentrate long enough to retrieve a particular word sound from memory. Similarly, a child trying to concentrate on a math problem may be unable to exercise selective attention. Unwanted thoughts and misinformation come crowding into his or her consciousness, like a dozen circus acts competing for space in the center ring. Doctors are better at diagnosing and treating ADHD than in the past, but a great deal is still unknown about this large category of learning disorders.

SPATIAL, MOTOR, AND OTHER
PERCEPTUAL DEFICITS

Many learning-disabled individuals manifest various spatial or motor-skill (muscle coordination) problems. They have difficulty judging their own bodies in relation to space and consequently seem clumsy and accident-prone. They may have poor motor coordination and balance or immature small-muscle control. They may stutter, and it may be hard for them to hold a pencil, draw, and cut with scissors. As children, they may be unusually slow to hop, skip, or run. It may be hard for these children to judge distances, and in a softball game the moving ball may seem closer than it really is, or first base may seem impossibly far away. A young child may think the slowly moving swing in the playground is moving far too fast or that a tricycle several feet away could run into him. To this child, sudden movement may be especially threatening. Such children are often teased for being "sissies" when in reality they simply perceive the world differently.

In addition to motor deficits, some children have difficulty developing social skills. The clues to social behavior that are obvious to most people somehow escape them. They may interrupt or talk too loudly and do not understand how to make friends. They are usually unaware of how others perceive their behavior. Often they have other learning disabilities, such as reading problems, that aggravate their antisocial behavior. Just as they have trouble decoding words, they may have trouble picking up on social clues such as body language and facial expressions. With counseling, children with this disability can learn social skills and recover their self-esteem.

Like other learning disabilities, social and motor deficits can easily be confused with normal delays in development. Parents often become unduly anxious if their baby has not yet learned to walk or if their seven year old cannot ride a two-wheeler. There are enormous variations in children's growth patterns, and slight delays beyond what many consider to be the "norm" are not necessarily a cause for concern to parents. If the delays persist, a skilled diagnostician can identify whether they suggest the presence of a learning disability.

•   •   •   •

CHAPTER 3

· · · · · · · · · · · · · · · ·

THE EVALUATION PROCESS

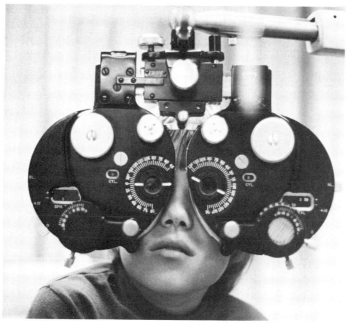

A boy undergoes an eye exam.

Most children with learning disabilities are diagnosed in elementary school, where the problem usually surfaces first. In most cases, the child was probably tested by completing puzzles, matching words with definitions, and listening to tapes.

Perhaps you yourself have just gone through testing for a learning disability and wonder what exactly the tests were all about—what they told the tester and whether or not you will be judged

33

by those tests for the remainder of your school years. First of all, the law requires that children with educational disabilities must be reevaluated every three years. The results of the tests are judged individually and then compared to previous tests so that any improvements can be recorded. As for the tests themselves, some measure native intelligence or aptitude (i.e., the level of intelligence that you were born with and developed yourself), some test your school achievement, and others test your emotional well-being. Many tests that evaluate learning problems were not designed specifically for that purpose. Rather, they were developed to assess the aptitude and achievement level of all schoolchildren. Thus, whether or not you have a learning disability, you have probably had to take one or more of these tests at some point in your life.

The process of diagnosing and evaluating a learning disability, unlike diagnosing the results of an X ray or throat culture, is not especially scientific. Aptitude and achievement tests give only an approximate measure of performance and of future capability. Therefore, the most accurate assessment of a learning problem includes a classroom observation, a parent interview, a medical report, and a psychological evaluation, all in addition to a variety of intelligence tests. A final evaluation is usually based on the

One of the most important components in deciding whether a child has a learning disability is a consultation involving a parent, the child, and his doctor.

conclusions of a team of diagnosticians, not on the judgment of just one tester.

Learning experts are well aware that external factors, many of them subject to change, influence the diagnosis of a learning disability. A child may improve as school anxiety lessens, family tensions are resolved, or developmental hurdles are overcome. It is because of these changeable factors that a new evaluation is required every three years and a review of the individual educational plan of each learning-disabled student is required every year.

As imperfect as the diagnostic process may be, it has substantial benefits. First, an early diagnosis of a learning problem can bring help before the problem worsens. Kindergarten or first grade is the best time to spot difficulties, before children begin to feel different from their classmates. Teachers and learning specialists emphasize that early diagnosis is often critical to future success. Emotional problems, such as loss of self-esteem, can so overwhelm a child that they, rather than any specific learning disorder, become the primary disability.

Second, a diagnosis of a learning disability qualifies a student to seek help from the school's learning-skills teachers or to switch to a smaller class. Sometimes the diagnostic team recommends a different school or psychiatric counseling. In any case, the student qualifies for an individualized educational plan. Federal law 94–142, which has been called an "educational bill of rights," ensures "free appropriate education" for all students with special needs. This law specifies that each learning-disabled student must have an individualized educational program (IEP) based on his or her needs and not limited to the resources of a particular teacher or classroom.

The IEP assesses a student's current strengths and weaknesses and outlines his or her reasonable short-term objectives and long-term goals. The program begins at the student's level of accomplishment and moves forward at the pace of the student, not the pace of the rest of the class. For example, a dyslexic student's reading objective over the course of a year might be learning to recognize a list of 20 new words, learning to divide words into syllables, and reading several books along with tape recordings. Long-term goals might include learning to type, asking for help, and accepting errors with less frustration.

(continued on page 38)

Two Parents' Points of View

MRS. S: Stevie's difficulties began when he was learning to read. I guess he would be called a slow learner. He was always a bit on the active side but not hyperactive. He has always felt different from the other kids. He's in seventh grade now and it's getting even harder. Kids don't want to feel they're different, especially in adolescence.

I am a divorced, single parent. That's exacerbated Stevie's problems. There are so many things I feel guilty about. Divorce breeds insecurity and guilt on both sides. His father is much more of a disciplinarian and finger pointer. It's hard on a kid.

We had Stevie tested at the end of second grade. The report was not terribly specific. They said his IQ was average to above average. They stressed that it would be important for him to go to a structured school and for us to be very consistent with him.

They also suggested the possible use of Ritalin because of his active nature. We had him tested again at another hospital and they were even more insistent about trying Ritalin.

I didn't want Stevie to be on a drug. I want my son to learn to control his activity himself. I feared the drug would inhibit his growth. So I just never considered it strongly. His activity level has decreased since he's gotten older. Socially he's a very adept child. He's also lucky because he's good at sports. But he really doesn't feel confident about his ability no matter what I tell him. Inside he doesn't believe he's capable if he's had to get all this help. I tell him you just have to work on it.

MRS. D: Chris was always a sweet kid—considerate. Of all my children, he gave me the least trouble. I returned to work when he was in the second grade. Shortly after that, we began to notice that he was having trouble. Spelling was difficult for him; math and reading were not easy either. On my nights off, I would sit with Chris and try to help him with his homework. It was a frustrating experience. By the end of the evening, I would ask him a question, but instead of answering me, he would just say, "I don't know." This would go on for hours. How do you spell this? "I don't know." What is 2 times 4? "I don't know." What is this word? "I don't know!"

His difficulties with math, I

thought, were understandable. I had never been very good with numbers, though my husband is. Our two other children grasped it easily, but Chris always struggled with it. I thought it must have been something he inherited from me—this math "dumbness." The rest, though, I began to think was just Chris's way of getting even with me for leaving him each afternoon to go to work. Even though he had an older brother and sister and his father usually came home two hours after school got out, I thought that my working had somehow interfered with Chris's schooling—maybe he wasn't getting enough help at home, maybe he just wasn't trying anymore.

Students suffering from ADHD, or attention deficit hyperactive disorder, may find it virtually impossible to sit still in class. Many physicians prescribe Ritalin for this condition.

Sometimes when I tried to help him, I would end up screaming, "You're not trying!" and poor Chris would start crying and scream, "I am! I'm just dumb!" and throw his book on the floor and run out.

At the end of that year, the parochial school Chris attended decided to leave him back. I was crushed, and so was Chris. Thank God, Chris's teacher finally spoke up. She told me she thought Chris was very bright—that perhaps he just had a learning disability. I didn't really know that much about learning disabilities, but my husband and I took Chris to be evaluated, and, sure enough, that's what it turned out to be.

In order to get the help he needed, we transferred Chris to a public school. There he worked with other children in a resource room to complete his homework and work out any tough problems. Chris had some trouble learning as fast as the other kids in a normal setting. Fortunately, he also had another wonderful teacher who was willing to stay after school with him and come in early to help with the topics they were covering in class.

During high school, Chris attended vocational classes in electricity along with his regular classwork. He soon found that he was really good at electric work—he was bringing home straight A's. Today, Chris is training to be an electrician. He has outgrown his learning disability and is never frustrated by things anymore. His life is really on track.

(continued from page 35)

The third and most important advantage of a detailed and careful diagnosis is that it provides students with invaluable information about themselves. The tests may point out strengths a student did not realize he or she possessed or had simply taken for granted. For this reason, it is crucial that the tester be alert for areas in which the learning-disabled student excels and not just for shortcomings.

The main purpose of the tests, however, is to identify areas that need strengthening. Armed with this information, the student can begin to ask for help on his or her own instead of relying on parents or teachers. Many students feel relieved when a name is given to their learning problems. Their frustration diminishes, and they are less likely to blame themselves. At the same time, they discover that teachers and parents are more sympathetic and patient once they realize that the the child was not simply "acting up," refusing to try, or willfully causing discipline problems. Consequently, as the student begins to receive help in coping with his or her problems, he or she also begins to feel more optimistic about the future.

DIAGNOSTIC TESTS

There are literally hundreds of tests that measure aptitude, achievement, vocational interests, auditory and visual perception, right- or left-handedness, mental health, and motor skills. And there are many tests that measure intelligence alone. But whereas tests and testing procedures differ from one school system to another, one test, the Wechsler Intelligence Scale for Children-Revised (WISC-R) stands out above all the rest. This is the test most commonly administered to children ages 6–16. A similar test, called the Wechsler Adult Intelligence Test, is administered to individuals age 16 and up.

It is extremely difficult to find a definition of intelligence that everyone will accept. But American psychologist David Wechsler, the researcher who developed the WISC-R test, managed to develop one that few people find objectionable. Wechsler defined intelligence as "the overall capacity of an individual to understand and cope with the world around him." Intelligence includes

A student completes a section of the WISC-R test. Students with learning disabilities generally score higher on the performance part of the test, which stresses visual perception, than they do on the verbal section.

learning from experience, solving problems, and adapting to change.

For the most part, people equate intelligence with school performance. Wechsler understood, however, that schoolwork involves only one part of the brain. The brain has two hemispheres, each specializing in a different way of thinking and learning. It is easier and much more common to test facts and figures (left-brain information) than to test visual comprehension and imagination (right-brain information). Wechsler found a way to test both hemispheres. His exam contains two parts, a verbal scale and a performance scale, each of which contains six subtests. The subtests of the verbal scale test vocabulary, comprehension, and knowledge. On the performance scale, the subtests include, among other things, sections on picture completion, in which a student is shown a series of pictures and asked to identify a part missing from each, and block design, in which a student must copy with blocks a series of designs printed on cards.

The results of the WISC-R subtests are averaged together to obtain an intelligence quotient, or IQ score. An average score is between 90 and 109; a score of 80–89 is considered low average and 110–119 high average. A score of 120–129 is superior, and

A young girl takes a block test to determine her visual perception.

130 and above is very superior. Most learning-disabled students do better on the performance scale, which requires nonverbal answers and tests visual perception. Because the WISC-R test is administered to very young children as well as high school students, the questions require little or no reading. The questions progress from very simple to quite difficult and cannot be prepared for beforehand. Some learning-disabled students do extremely poorly on the verbal subtests and extremely well on performance subtests. The final averaged score will not show these differences, so it is important that the student or his or her parents ask for a breakdown of the results.

Even with the diversity in testing material, the WISC-R is not a perfect test. For one thing it tests more left-brain than right-brain strengths. And, like most IQ tests, it does not measure an individual's innate potential to learn or willingness to persevere in solving a problem. Also, although the test is designed so as not to be economically, culturally, or racially discriminatory, a certain cultural environment is an obvious advantage for anyone taking the test, especially for such sections as vocabulary.

The more serious a student's disability, the more tests he or she will probably have to take. Each test adds another piece of information, helping learning specialists understand how a student learns best. There is the Wide Range Achievement Test (WRAT), the Spache Oral Diagnostic Reading Test, the Gates MacGinitie Silent Reading Test, the Marianne Frostig Developmental Test of Visual Perception, the Detroit Test of Learning Aptitude, and more. The method of scoring differs for all these tests. Some scores, especially for younger children, are given by mental age. For example, a mental-age score of 10 years, 9 months indicates a performance level typical of a student of that age. Other scores are by percentile—a score in the 58th percentile means a performance is as good as or better than that registered by 58 out of every 100 students tested. The percentile may be based on national scores or on the scores of a local school district.

Children with hearing problems are often mistakenly believed to be learning disabled. A simple hearing test such as the one shown here can determine the root of the problem.

A *stanine* score ranges from a low of 1 to a high of 9, with 5 as the average.

In addition to the testing, a medical examination often is necessary to rule out any hearing, vision, or nutritional problems. Occasionally, a neurologist (a physician specializing in brain functions) will conduct further tests that measure speech articulation (clarity of word pronunciation), coordination and balance, memory, and fine-motor performance (skills such as writing, sewing, and using scissors). A psychiatric examination often is required to determine how the student's learning is hindered by emotional problems such as poor self-esteem or family problems such as financial worries or alcoholism.

In order to find more reliable and uniform diagnostic methods, researchers are currently working to perfect the testing process for learning disabilities. According to a February 1988 article in the *New York Times*, these researchers are making some interesting discoveries. For example, Dr. Anneliese A. Pontius, a neuropsychiatrist at Harvard Medical School, discovered that most spatial dyslexics draw human faces with no separation of the nose from the forehead and with no nose bridge. Dr. Pontius describes this drawing pattern as "neolithic." She compared these drawings to the drawings of prehistoric or preliterate people and found that they were actually quite similar. Another new test has been developed by Dr. Martin F. Gardiner of the Harvard Medical School. In this test, the student is asked to tap his or her finger on a table. A person without a learning disability can easily tap out a rhythm according to spoken instructions, but a spatial dyslexic cannot. The dyslexic may understand the instructions; he or she simply cannot carry them out. According to Dr. Gardiner, test results suggest that the region in the brain responsible for spatial abilities may be closely related to the region responsible for musical ability.

These tests do not conclusively prove what causes certain learning disabilities, but they do provide scientists with a starting point for further research. Indeed, all the various tests and the many different theories put forth to explain learning disabilities all lead toward one common element—the human brain.

•   •   •   •

CHAPTER 4

· · · · · · · · · · · · · · · ·

WHAT CAUSES LEARNING DISABILITIES?

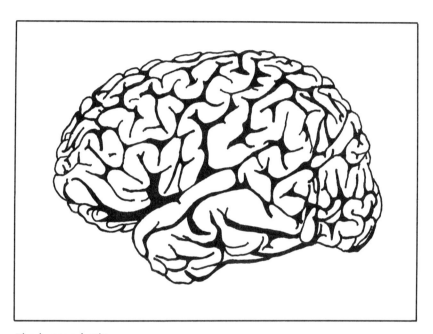

The human brain.

Learning disabilities have no single or primary cause. Rather, they evolve from a combination of biologic and environmental influences. Thus, their causes are more difficult to isolate than the causes of a physical illness like the flu. Flu cases differ in type and severity, but microscopic examination of a throat culture can determine the particular strain of virus responsible for a patient's high fever. In the case of learning disabilities, however, there is rarely an instance in which a single cause can be found

43

and all others ruled out. And of the various possible causes, the most intriguing lie within the brain.

The brain was where Dr. Hinshelwood thought reading problems developed. In the 1890s he observed that adults with brain injuries often suffered from dysfunctional reading problems similar to those of children with reading problems. He theorized that "acquired word-blindness" in adults and "congenital [existing from birth] word-blindness" in children were both caused by damage to language-related centers in the brain. In other words, if the symptoms of reading difficulty were the same in children as in adults, the cause was probably the same. Unfortunately, he had no proof to support his theories.

Lack of scientific evidence for Hinshelwood's theory did not prevent later researchers from believing he was right. Orton, the American neurologist mentioned previously, examined patients with reading difficulties and concluded that their problems originated in the brain's left hemisphere, the brain's language center. Orton believed the left hemisphere was dominant in most readers but that dyslexics had mixed dominance, causing letter reversals, for which he coined the now defunct term *strephosymbolia*. Today's neuroscientists continue to dissect and probe the convoluted interior of the brain to find exactly what in its cross-circuitry might cause various learning disabilities.

Uncovering the Mysteries of the Brain

In the course of their work, scientists examining the causes of learning disabilities have gained a better understanding of the brain's composition. The average brain weighs about three pounds, though its weight and size varies from one human being to another and has no bearing on intelligence. The organ is made up of millions of neuron cells that, in turn, make up nerve tissue and transmit and receive nerve impulses. Each cell consists of a cell body from which axons and dendrites (nerve matter that relays impulses away from and to nerve cells) branch out to connect with other cells. The synapse, or the point at which nerve impulses are transmitted, is located between the axons and the dendrites.

This great network of neurons is divided into specialized areas. The hindbrain, which includes the cerebellum, is the oldest, most primitive part, existing in humans far longer than any other region of the brain. The midbrain, or old mammalian brain, developed next. The forebrain, including the cerebral cortex, is the largest and most advanced area of the brain. The cerebral cortex is responsible for controlled motor functions, sensory perception, speech, memory, and emotions—all the complex responses that make us human beings.

The cerebral cortex is organized into two hemispheres—the left hemisphere and the right hemisphere—that are connected by an important bundle of nerve fibers called the corpus callosum. The left hemisphere contains areas specialized in the production and comprehension of language and is associated with orderly, precise thinking. The right hemisphere contains areas specialized in visual perception, music, and emotions and is associated with instinctive and nonverbal responses. The two hemispheres must work together, in cooperation with motor and sensory areas of the cortex, to create intelligent speech and written language or mathematics.

When a person has suffered a stroke, a rupture or obstruction of an artery in the brain, in 95% of the cases the resultant speech

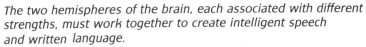

The two hemispheres of the brain, each associated with different strengths, must work together to create intelligent speech and written language.

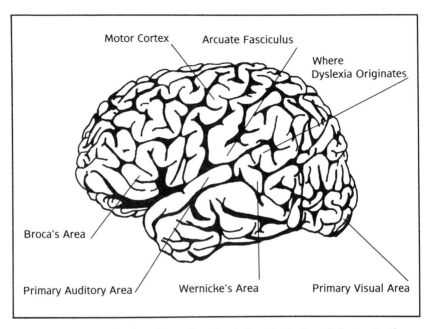

Motor Cortex   Arcuate Fasciculus

Where
Dyslexia Originates

Broca's Area

Primary Auditory Area   Wernicke's Area   Primary Visual Area

In recent years scientists have theorized that dyslexia originates in the left hemisphere of the brain, where unusual arrangements of neurons have been found.

and reading disturbances stem from damage that has occurred in the language areas of the left hemisphere. According to an article in *Scientific American*, there have been many cases in which damage to the left hemisphere has left stroke victims unable to talk but able to sing. Also, the stroke victim may sink into severe depression. When damage occurs to the right hemisphere, however, the stroke victim is apt to be unconcerned about his or her condition. He or she may lack appropriate emotional responses and fail to perceive other people's emotions.

As a result of ongoing research, scientists now have a better idea of how the brain functions. At one time, scientists believed a single cell could be responsible for storing a particular piece of information—the date of your mother's birthday, for example. But, according to a June 1988 article in the *Boston Globe*, recent experiments conducted at the University of California with epileptic patients have shown that a network of individual cells will burst into activity to recognize a particular word, date, fact, or face. It was also once believed that the left brain was far more important than the right. Today, however, scientists suspect they have long underestimated the importance and potential of the right hemisphere of the brain. They now have a better appreciation for the interdependency of both areas of the brain.

Although the two halves of the brain look symmetrical, in most people they are slightly different in size. Some of these size differences, or asymmetries, are apparent in the rear portion of the left hemisphere, an area specifically used for language. Normal brain asymmetry suggests that in most people the left hemisphere is dominant over the right hemisphere. In a measurement study of 337 brain specimens, 70% showed asymmetry favoring the left hemisphere (meaning this hemisphere is larger). This asymmetry can be detected even before birth in a human fetus. In dyslexic brains the two hemispheres often are much more equal in size. This equality has led scientists to speculate, as Orton did, that many learning-disabled people have "mixed dominance," though exactly how this might cause their learning problems is unknown.

Scientists are uncovering more and more evidence of differences between the brains of learning-disabled people, especially dyslexics, and others. In the brain tissue of dyslexics, neurologists

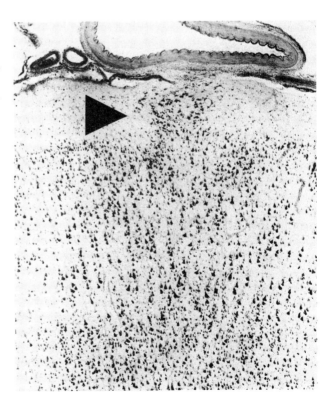

In this dyslexia patient, a cluster of nerve cells (arrow) is found protruding into the outermost layer of the cerebral cortex. Normally there are no nerve cells found in this area.

have observed unusual arrangements of neurons that look like disorganized networks, or "clouds," of cells. Some cell patterns look disrupted, and others show the presence of nerve cells that are normally absent. Neurologists have also noted that the nerve fibers of the corpus callosum, connecting the two hemispheres, are more numerous and disorganized in dyslexics than in most other people. In other words, instead of having fewer brain cells, many learning-disabled individuals have too many. These extra nerve fibers, which normally die off during fetal development, seem to inhibit learning and concentration. Some scientists speculate that an excess of antibodies (substances unleashed by the body's immune system to fight off infection and disease) from the mother during pregnancy may cause this difference in brain development. However, many scientists suggest that research results are too limited or contradictory to link any of these anatomical differences with learning problems such as dyslexia, especially in young people.

By studying the flow of blood through the brain, neurologists have observed yet another difference. As reported in a December 1987 article in the *New York Times*, when most people are asked to read something, the right and left hemispheres are equally active. But, according to Dr. Judith Rumsey of the National Institute of Mental Health, when people with dyslexia are asked to read, the left hemisphere becomes more active than the right hemisphere. Instead of not working hard enough, certain areas of the left hemisphere seem to work extra hard, though less efficiently. Researchers have also identified an area of the midtemporal lobe, necessary for visual discrimination, that is more active in dyslexics when they read than in other people.

A sophisticated technology called brain electrical activity mapping, or BEAM, suggests still more differences. In a BEAM study, electrodes (small, round disks that conduct electricity) taped to a volunteer's scalp record brain responses to such tasks as reading, listening to music, or memorizing numbers. The increased attention required for these tasks usually activates faster brain waves. Alpha waves, those that help us relax, usually slow down. Researchers discovered that in a small number of dyslexic subjects alpha waves in the frontal lobes remained just as active or even increased their activity during tasks demanding high concentration. However, other BEAM researchers have not noted this same alpha-wave difference, which suggests that some of the dyslexic subjects may have simply failed to pay adequate attention to the task. Research in this area is still being conducted.

A central aspect of dyslexia and of ADHD is an inability to concentrate and pay attention. Scientists contend that this failure may be caused by a deficiency in certain brain chemicals called neurotransmitters (chemicals that transmit nerve impulses across synapses). Without adequate neurotransmitters, the centers of the brain that control behavior and attention cannot work properly.

To understand how the brain works and what might go wrong, imagine the organ as a highly advanced computer. The more parts it has, the more can go wrong and the harder it becomes to locate the source of the problem. Sometimes a glitch occurs in the computer circuitry, as, for example, when the circuits become damaged by a surge of electricity or if the short-term memory is not sufficiently developed. Information gets lost, and the retrieval system breaks down; too many signals are sent to the printer, which cannot sort through them to print the message. You might also imagine the brain as a telephone switchboard. When too many signals come in at once, the lines get overloaded.

In addition to the findings of neurologists, there is further evidence that biology plays an important role in causing learning problems. Researchers have long noted that some learning problems seem to be inherited. Now they have found a genetic explanation for this. A group of scientists at the University of Colorado in Denver including J. C. DeFuies, David Fulker, and Michele La Buda, studied 119 sets of identical and fraternal twins. At least one member of each pair had reading problems. Thirty percent of the cases where both twins had reading problems showed that there was a defect on chromosome 15, one of the 23 pairs of chromosomes that carry the genetic matter we inherit from our parents. Another study conducted by Dr. Herbert Cubs of the University of Miami, Shelly Smith of Boys Town National Institute in Omaha, and Bruce Pennington of the University of Colorado Medical Center in Denver, concluded that 1 out of 3 cases of inherited dyslexia can be linked to a defect on

A relatively high percentage of learning-disabled people are left-handed.

chromosome 15. Scientists suspect that under certain conditions this defective gene can sometimes—but not always—cause a specific brain malfunction.

There are additional reasons to look for biologic causes of learning problems. Some disabilities, in particular ADHD, often respond well to drug therapy. Because stimulant drugs such as methylphenidate (brand name Ritalin) effect a positive physiological response in ADHD patients, researchers have concluded that ADHD must have a physiological foundation. Biologic causes would also seem to explain why many learning-disabled individuals have problems with motor coordination, poor vision, allergies, or stuttering.

Finally, according to an article in *Scientific American*, researchers are fascinated by an apparent association between learning problems and handedness. They note that only 9% of the human population is left-handed but that a much higher proportion of learning-disabled people are left-handed. The left hand is controlled by the right side of the brain, a finding that suggests learning-disabled people are more "right-brained" than others.

Sometimes learning deficits have an environmental cause. Lead-paint poisoning in young children can cause behavioral

Many scientists believe that a poor diet, one high in sugar and artificial preservatives, can impair ones attention span and cause learning problems.

disorders, neurological damage, mental retardation, and even death. It is a tragic consequence of poverty, inadequate housing, and neglect. A poor diet or consistent lack of sleep can also impair attention and cause learning problems.

A pediatrician named Benjamin Feingold theorized that food additives such as food coloring, preservatives, excessive sugar, and artificial flavorings can cause hyperactivity and other learning problems. Research based on Feingold's theory shows mixed and inconsistent results, although one study reported that a small number of children did benefit from an additive-free diet. At the time of this printing, there remained more than 3,000 food additives that had not been tested for their effects on behavior.

Differences in Brain Development

For all that is known about the brain, there is a vast amount that remains mysterious, including the exact reason why some brains are so different from others. Scientists know, however, that brain differences do not show up among all learning-disabled individuals. Many dyslexic brains look like other brains. Thus, though their findings are exciting, neurologists do not believe there is a biologic basis for all learning problems. Finally, with the notable exception of genetics research, most research has been limited to the dissection of dead brains and work with stroke victims, epileptics, or adult dyslexics. Neurologists can only speculate as to how their findings with these subjects relate to the origins of learning problems in schoolchildren.

Other scientists maintain that it is not necessarily a matter of different brain chemistry, or genetics, but rather a result of disturbances in the environment that cause learning disabilities. The next chapter examines these theories and the explanations they offer for the development of learning disorders.

•   •   •   •

CHAPTER 5

· · · · · · · · · · · · · · ·

ENVIRONMENTAL FACTORS

Most of us remember information easily when it has positive associations. A best friend's phone number, the winning score in a victorious ball game, the lyrics of a favorite song—all tend to stay with us. On the other hand, the due date for a dreaded book report or the subplot of a dull and difficult novel may totally defeat our powers of recollection. The reason for the discrepancy is that psychological, environmental, and emotional factors influence our ability to acquire and retrieve information. The connection is reasonable, given that the centers that control our emotions and our intellect are seated side by side in the brain.

In the Middle Ages, people believed that the heart was the seat of the emotions. And today, although we know better, we commonly relate feelings to the heart, perhaps because we secretly wish the messy entanglements of anger, discouragement, and sadness were located at a safe distance from our mental activities. If this were indeed the case, no fear of past failure could disturb our concentration on an algebra problem, and, during a high-pressure exam, tension would not slow the flow of information from our memory to our fingers as they tightly grip a pen.

Unfortunately, reality does not conform to our wishes. Students know all too well how much their emotions, their psychological state, and the outside environment influence their mental activity. It seems obvious that the atmosphere in which we study has a great deal to do with what we learn and how well we learn it. Thus, no one chooses a school or college simply on the basis of how many books are contained in its library; instead, we examine the whole picture of campus life for enthusiastic students and caring teachers.

But can emotional and environmental factors actually cause a learning disability? Many researchers believe they can and argue that the psychological component of learning is so strong that in combination certain key factors can cause major learning difficulties. Others argue that more often psychological factors exacerbate existent learning problems and can, for instance, turn a slow reader into a disabled reader. Still others see environmental and psychological factors as having only a small influence on such serious learning problems as spatial dyslexia.

Most people speculate from time to time about the effects—subtle or obvious—that their environment has had on their ability to learn. No one knows for sure how much of an effect these factors have. It would be unfair to put all the blame for a reading disorder on an older sibling, a parent, a recent move across the country, or a few bad teachers. Many people have survived worse situations and not suffered learning problems. But each person reacts to events and situations differently, and each person's way of learning probably results from the interplay between minute neurological factors and environmental and psychological influences.

Although it is seldom possible to identify a single cause when tracing the origins of a learning disability, the following can affect a person's success in absorbing and retaining knowledge.

THE SCHOOL

Because most learning disabilities surface only after children first enter the classroom, schools are the most obvious places to begin looking for factors that discourage learning. They can be difficult to detect, especially in the best schools, whose administrators and teachers resist the notion that the environment they have worked hard to create might be damaging to a student. Educators are likely to assume the fault lies in the "slow" student's innate ability to learn.

The problem, in part, lies with the educational system itself. Teachers receive an established curriculum in September that they must complete by June. And students must keep up. In addition, although few students learn in exactly the same way or at the same pace, most classrooms are based on the assumption that they do. When students are first learning to read, for example, those who need extra time or a better explanation of something often miss critical information and have no opportunity to make up the loss later.

When children are first learning to read, those who need extra help or who move at a slower pace often miss crucial information and fall behind the rest of the class.

In even the most nurturing school environment, these methods influence how well a child learns to read. In fact, most schools use a combination of methods when teaching children how to read. The phonetic method teaches the sound of each letter and combination of letters. The "look and say" method encourages recognition of the whole word through repetition and association with pictures. Some teachers rely exclusively on one method, others combine the two. Both have their advantages and their drawbacks. Children with good visual recognition usually grasp the "look and say" method but may struggle with phonetics because they cannot distinguish different vowel and consonant sounds. On the other hand, children who are not taught phonetics may forever lack an ability to sound out and recognize unfamiliar words. These children often have trouble progressing beyond an elementary reading level.

Most reading instruction includes a time when children take turns reading aloud. This can be a painful exercise for slow or shy readers. If the teacher is quick to correct errors, young children may grow discouraged. The ordeal is compounded by reading texts with implausible characters and tedious plots that are often dull and even insulting to young readers. The children perceive that the text is not a "real" book but, rather, one designed solely to teach them reading. These factors combine to make children regard reading as a chore rather than a potentially life-long pleasure.

Developmental differences also create handicaps in the classroom. The age requirements for entrance to first grade are the same for girls and boys, but most six-year-old boys are less mature than most six-year-old girls and thus are not as ready for formal schooling. Consequently, they may miss important reading instruction because they have not yet developed adequate attention and concentration skills.

A host of other school-related factors can impede learning. In the typical special-education class, there is not enough communication between learning specialists and classroom teachers. Also, in a highly competitive school and community, teachers and parents sometimes set unrealistic goals for young people. If many children in a community perform above the average level, a child of "average" ability may be wrongly diagnosed as disabled.

From peekaboo games of infancy, a host of factors influence learning development. Parents have the greatest impact on this development, providing most of the stimuli and reinforcement that will shape it.

THE FAMILY

The first place where children learn is not at school but in the home, where they compete with siblings, play with toys, and share experiences with friends. It is at home that they learn to perceive themselves as either capable or incompetent. From the first "peekaboo" game of infancy, a host of factors influence learning development. Parents have the greatest influence on this development, but siblings, relatives, and the general atmosphere of the home also contribute to a child's view of him- or herself.

Some parents are permissive, others are authoritarian. Most fall somewhere in between. It is difficult to gauge when parental behavior might harm a child's ability to learn. Parents can hamper a child by being overprotective, anxious, and controlling— organizing and supervising their children's games, rebuilding the

(continued on page 60)

Profile #2: "The Lines Would Seem to Separate"

Jon, 18, is tall and thin, with dark hair. His expression is serious as he talks about himself. He has just graduated from a private boarding school that specializes in helping students with learning problems.

"In elementary school I started having trouble with reading. My eyes would wander. The lines would seem to separate. I had problems with math, too. I can't memorize all the formulas and what they do. Before sixth grade my Mom would help me. She read to me a lot. But in sixth grade it started getting harder. My Mom couldn't do all the math, and I started having to write more papers. I had trouble getting my ideas down in the right way. My reading wasn't good. I had a lot of trouble pronouncing words.

"The public school wasn't any help, so we had to get private tutors. We asked friends whose kids had tutors. Throughout school I've needed an enormous amount of help and tutoring.

"There were other factors, too. I've moved around so much that I've had to get used to different kids all the time. I would make a lot of friends and then I'd have to leave them. My stepfather was into real estate, and we had a campground in Florida. Then he thought there was more land in Colorado, so we moved there. Then we traveled to New York City so he could take over his father's business. I would say that moving was 40% of my handicap. I was 15 when we moved to New York. I was angry about that move.

"My family is confusing. I was adopted as an infant. My Mom got divorced and she remarried when I was three. Now I have one sister, three stepsisters, and one stepbrother.

"I'm a good skier. I started skiing when I was 10 and learned faster than anyone else in my fam-

Many learning-disabled students find it helpful to listen to a tape while reading the same passage in a book.

ily. I can pick up sports easily. In academics, if I stick to something, I usually get it done. I work hard. I like talking to people and helping them with problems. I'm also pretty neat and organized.

"I'm not good at time management. I used to have a lot of trouble with studying. My class participation was poor. I really don't like to read books. Reading with tapes has helped me a lot.

"Boarding school has also helped. I had to learn to deal with things on my own because before my Mom had always been there for me. At the boarding school we had a schedule every day and a mandatory study hall from seven to nine every evening. If you weren't studying, they would ask you what was the matter. The students had the same kinds of problems. We were all in the same boat and didn't feel ashamed of it.

"I don't want people to think that if they have a learning problem they're stupid. They may just have a slower way of learning. There are people who can help you, but you have to ask for help. You can't expect it to come to you. You have to learn to deal with it and live with it. You have to just accept that it's a problem that you have and be happy with yourself."

(continued from page 57)

block castle when it falls down, finding the missing puzzle piece, and correcting homework before it is handed in to the teacher. This extreme involvement does not teach the child perseverance or self-reliance, nor does the child learn that it is a normal part of learning to make mistakes and profit from them. At the opposite extreme are neglectful parents who are sometimes so preoccupied with their own problems that they cannot give their children the love and self-confidence they need to succeed in school.

Parents often make unrealistic demands on the firstborn child and baby a younger child. This discrepancy may breed competitive feelings between the siblings. Sometimes a parent who is dissatisfied with his or her own career compensates by placing unrealistic expectations on a son or daughter. Financial stress can also make parents resent their responsibility for their children's future. They may fear, for instance, that they cannot afford college tuition for their child, who therefore must get good enough grades to qualify for a scholarship. The child, in turn, may feel that academic success is the only way to please such parents. But anxiety about reaching that goal is apt to make it hard to concentrate on schoolwork and can lead to behavior problems. Divorce, illness, or a death in the family can also cause enough anxiety to disrupt learning.

Long before kindergarten or first grade, children should be introduced to books at home. In the secure comfort of a parent's lap, they can discover the joy of being read to and the beauty of language and the imagination. But many parents themselves do not read and never acquaint their children with books.

The home is also the place where a child develops study habits. It helps to have a regular time at which to study and a regular location—a desk in a bedroom or the dining-room table. It also helps to have as models parents, friends, or older siblings concentrating on homework, tax forms, crossword puzzles, correspondence, or reading. A child is not likely to value learning and concentration if the television is always blaring and a set of headphones is constantly providing background music.

•   •   •   •

CHAPTER 6

. . . .

TREATMENT

Diagraming sentences at the Gow School.

It is fascinating to speculate on the cause of learning disabilities, but what matters to most people who suffer from them is getting treatment and finding a way to cope. For children, coping can mean acquiring skills that enable them to read, developing resources that allow them to remain in the classroom with their peers, or mastering techniques that restore their self-esteem. For older students, coping can mean finding a school geared exclusively to learning-disabled students or a college program sensitive to their particular needs. For learning-disabled adults, coping can mean balancing independence with the aid provided by a support group, landing a job that uses their skills without highlighting their weaknesses, or gaining a skill that allows them to check their work for certain recurrent errors.

Luckily, many of these needs are being met today, and many different options are open to the learning disabled. Each option addresses a different disability or degree of disability, and each is designed to help people of different age groups and academic levels. Treatment often involves more than one strategy. It is not enough to place a student in a better school or in smaller classes if his or her family continues to be unsupportive; nor will family therapy alone help if the child is physically incapable of sitting still and concentrating in class.

Whether the cause of a learning problem is primarily physiologic or environmental, both need full consideration when it comes to treatment. The next two chapters explore the different treatment options available to people with learning disabilities, from medication and school programs to psychotherapy and independent living programs. In this chapter, treatment strategies will be divided roughly between those that treat an organic, biologic cause and those that focus on the student's school environment, home life, or state of mind.

Although excessive reliance on drugs has recently come under fire, some drug treatments are often favored by specialists when the cause of a learning disability seems biologic. An oft-prescribed form of medication is amphetamines, which stimulate the nervous system and are prescribed most frequently to control hyperactivity and treat ADHD. Methylphenidate, known commonly by the brand name Ritalin, is used most often; Cylert (brand name for pemoline) and Dexedrine (brand name for dextroamphetamine) are prescribed less often. It may seem paradoxical that stimulant drugs should help young people who already seem overactive. However, the hyperactivity of ADHD children stems from their inability to focus their attention. Stimulant drugs can increase their attention focus and reduce unfocused hyperactivity. The student is thus enabled to concentrate on a task, to stop drumming on the desk, to listen to the teacher and to classmates—often for the first time. The drug usually becomes effective within half an hour, reaches its peak effectiveness within two hours, and is excreted from the body within four hours.

Ritalin is typically first prescribed in children of elementary-school age, the age when ADHD is often first diagnosed, although the ailment is increasingly being diagnosed in teenagers and adults, who also find Ritalin effective. Some children take the drug for only a few years, others for seven or eight. As their nervous systems mature, many young people outgrow their need for medication.

Amphetamine drugs have been used to control hyperactivity since about 1938, when Dexedrine was first introduced. Ritalin was introduced about 20 years later. Recently, Ritalin's effectiveness in improving academic achievement has come under closer scrutiny. Most current research shows that the drug can have a powerful influence on the academic learning of ADHD patients, especially in the first months of treatment. However, treatment must be carefully monitored for correct dosage, and most doctors prefer to begin treatment with the smallest possible dose, about 5 mg. Most physicians try to discontinue drug treatment before their patients reach puberty, because there is some evidence that the drug can suppress growth.

A teacher at Landmark helps two students with their lab work. Laboratory experimentation is ideal for learning-disabled students because it enables the students to strengthen right-hemisphere skills.

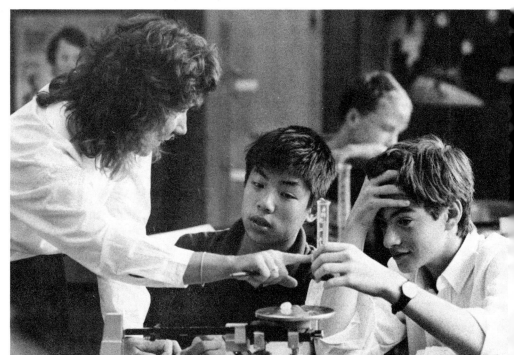

Some users of Ritalin suffer other side effects, although they are not very common. Patients have reported reduced appetite, headaches, and insomnia. There is some disagreement among researchers as to whether patients can build up a tolerance to the drug and others like it, in which case its benefits would disappear. Scientists stress, however, that Ritalin does not seem to predispose patients to drug abuse later in life.

Students for whom Ritalin has been prescribed often worry that their peers may discern that they are taking drugs and treat them differently. In fact, people cannot tell when someone is being treated with Ritalin. Moreover, if the student is better able to concentrate and, in turn, gains self-esteem, others may respond by being friendlier than before. Ritalin, however, is not a magic potion that can be taken to win friends or gain confidence. Rather, the ability to do so comes from within the learning-disabled student, not from any external source.

A student whose life improves after he or she takes the drug may ask him- or herself: "Is this the real me? Why couldn't people accept me as I was before?" The student may even resent that he or she has suddenly won acceptance after having been ignored or, worse yet, tormented for his or her disability. However, most students and their parents come to realize that this "new" person has been there all along and simply has not had the opportunity to develop or be recognized.

By 1988, Ritalin therapy had become the subject of fierce public controversy. Various parents' groups and religious organizations argued that psychiatrists relied too much on drugs to solve discipline problems and, as a result, overmedicated children. Processed foods and artificial flavors were blamed for causing hyperactivity, as was too much sugar. (These theories are not respected by most scientists.) Opponents of Ritalin suggested that other treatments, such as megavitamins and restricted diets, be tried first. Pointing to the fact that Ritalin sales had doubled in past years, these concerned adults feared that drug therapy was becoming a common classroom practice. In Massachusetts, lawyers defending a youth convicted of killing a classmate with a baseball bat argued that withdrawal from Ritalin made the boy more aggressive. As of 1988, at least eight medical malpractice suits had been filed against the drug.

Students with learning disabilities respond well to a highly structured classroom setting.

There is no question that Ritalin, like any other psychoactive drug, is at risk of being abused or mismanaged. Physicians, though they admit there are cases when the drug is not used correctly, suggest that most problems with Ritalin lie with the misdiagnosis of the children for whom it is prescribed. The drug may be wrongly prescribed when attention deficits or hyperactivity result not from a chemical deficiency but from bad parenting or the wrong school. However, other physicians maintain that Ritalin is not prescribed often enough. They claim that when used judiciously, with appropriate diagnosis, educational support, and psychotherapy, it is an extremely effective therapy.

A biologic approach to treatment also suggests using different teaching methods. Different teaching methods can be effective in treating learning problems, whether of biologic or environmental origin. In the typical high school classroom, students learn from lectures, textbooks, and mimeographed work sheets. There is heavy reliance on words and numbers, on getting the one "correct" answer, on organizing information in precise order.

(continued on page 68)

Profile #3: "My Self-Esteem Is Strong Now"

Michael, age 19, is from Brookline, Massachusetts. He has a thin face and frame and dark hair. Like many other learning-disabled people, he speaks slowly and thoughtfully. A high school graduate, Michael has spent the past year at a college that specifically serves the needs of learning disabled students.

"My dyslexia was diagnosed in second grade. They took me out of class and put me in a learning center. I didn't notice anything different in the way I learned until sixth or seventh grade. That's when the school sort of lost me. That's when they started helping me do the regular classwork. I was in a learning center (for learning-disabled students) for one or two blocks of the day. My self-esteem was lowest in seventh grade. Even though they knew about my learning problems, they didn't think I was working hard enough. My parents were supportive though. I'm an only child—I don't know if that makes a difference.

"I didn't go to the eighth grade. I had gotten such a bad report

A learning-disabled student works on a word processor. Computers have proven to be valuable educational tools for many such students.

card. My grades were really down, so I left regular school. They mainly did home tutoring for me that year. I told my friends I was going to another school. I just didn't want to say I was being tutored.

"Then they sent me to a special school. I thought I would be with kids with problems similar to mine, but the problems were runaways, drug addiction. I didn't have friends. I stayed there two and a half years, then started to go to a few high school classes. I took math and English.

"My senior year was one of my best years. I was at the high school full time. I spent two periods in the learning-skills room last year and took regular English and regular math. The way it normally goes at the high school is you go to a regular basic class and then you get additional help in the learning-skills room. Some teachers try not to let you get that help. Some teachers think students cheat in the learning skills room, but they don't.

"With dyslexia you usually have high intelligence but can't always express it in written language, so in turn people view you as dumb, as slow, or as lazy and lacking motivation. It's really quite annoying. If you go to write a note for somebody, you have to try to make it so they can read it. Or you have to explain.

"My writing is good but not my spelling. The thoughts that come out are good but only I can read them. For me it takes a long time to write an essay. I have a computer with a 'sensible speller' program. Now they have all kinds of programs: thesaurus, synonyms, homonyms.

"I liked reading Hemingway in high school, but I have a hard time keeping my concentration. Vonnegut is pretty interesting. That's what I did my senior paper on. But I pretty much never just pick up a novel.

"I like photography. I think I do pretty well at it. We have a dark room at our house because we used to do photo finishing. My father owns a store and I'm working at the store this summer.

"I try to read the *Wall Street Journal* every day. I've always been interested in business, marketing, even stocks maybe. Advertising is an interesting field.

"I'd like to go to a different college that's not just for the learning disabled. Being with all dyslexics is a kind of crutch. People use it as an excuse. I saw a lot of kids this year who really needed to be there, but I think a regular college with a good LD program would be better for me. Some colleges have fake LD programs, just to get the athletes by. You have to be careful. Every college has its sales pitch. On the surface it's hard to tell about a college unless you talk to a student who's been there.

"My self-esteem is strong now. I realize that I can do things. But that feeling has to come from yourself."

(continued from page 65)

These tasks rely heavily on left-hemisphere thinking, and most teachers are trained to teach primarily in this way. But this approach neglects the right hemisphere, the part of the brain that specializes in visual images and creative problem solving.

Many ordinary teaching techniques, however, can bring right-hemisphere thinking into the classroom. One high school had students who were studying molecular structure make models of different types of atoms using balls of Styrofoam, clay, and colored toothpicks. In another course, students having trouble with grammar were asked to imagine themselves as nouns, adverbs, and other parts of speech and to act out how they would interact. Laboratory experimentation, field trips, fantasy, role playing, and sensory stimulation all develop right-hemisphere strengths. Whenever possible, teachers should illustrate new information with colored diagrams and charts, use vivid metaphors to help students picture ideas in their minds, and encourage students to work "hands on" with real objects instead of merely reading about them. None of these techniques is uncommon, but many schools consider them secondary to textbook learning.

There are also occasions when a school or teacher is unwilling or unable to change teaching methods. If a learning problem seems to stem at least in part from a problem with the school itself—with the environment, in other words—the most drastic solution is to change schools. This is not a realistic choice for most families, who are then left only with the alternative of changing teachers.

School Programs, Resources, and Learning Disabilities

School systems differ enormously in their resources for helping learning-disabled students. Naturally, a well-funded school with a small number of disabled students and a staff committed to understanding and treating the problem will succeed better than a poorly funded school with an overwhelming number of disabled students. Federal law mandates, however, that each school system provide for the needs of all students—regardless of cost. The following treatment strategies have been helpful for many learning-disabled students:

Teachers at Landmark discuss students' IEPs—or individual education plans. The purpose of an IEP is to plan learning goals based on the student's abilities and not on those of his or her classmates.

1. A highly structured classroom setting. In such a class, students have a regular routine and schedule. Learning materials are easily accessible, well organized, and stored in the same place each day. Students know from day to day what is expected of them.

2. Easy, clear, and accessible assignments. These assignments are mimeographed or written on the blackboard as well as presented orally. Long assignments involving several steps are broken down into simpler steps.

3. Assignment flexibility—allowing a student with reading problems to listen to a tape of a novel or textbook while reading along with the book. Instead of handing in a written report, the student might be asked to prepare material orally, to put it on audiotape, or to illustrate it with graphics.

4. Testing flexibility—allowing untimed tests or oral test taking.

5. Special classes and learning centers. These offer intensive tutoring at the student's ability level. Some students spend the full school day in such classes; others attend a combination of special tutorial classes and regular classes.

6. A close partnership between special-education teachers, tutors, and regular classroom teachers.

7. An individualized educational plan. Such a plan is sometimes required by federal law and is drawn up by a team of special-education teachers and counselors. The plan outlines learning goals that are determined by the student's ability and not by the ability of his or her classmates.

8. An ungraded system of promotion based on the goals set by the individualized educational plan.

9. A relaxed, positive, safe school atmosphere.

Most of these strategies can help all students, not just the learning disabled. A growing number of teachers now enroll in special courses that explain how to understand the different ways their students learn and to implement more advanced teaching methods.

Though the situation is improving, few schools can offer learning-disabled young people all the help they need. Schools struggle to satisfy a great variety of students. Typically, there is a shortage of teachers and funds. Because many communities have limited resources, several private schools have been founded for the specific purpose of teaching students who learn differently. Colleges have also begun special learning programs. Similarly, independent living programs offer some disabled students the opportunity to live on their own and become contributing members of society. The next chapter examines some of these schools and programs and explores the benefits of each.

•   •   •   •

CHAPTER 7

• • • • • • • • • • • • • • • • •

SCHOOLS AND PROGRAMS

A student participates in Watermark.

As we have already seen, there are many new programs designed to benefit the learning-disabled student. Each program varies in intensity and specifics. Some try to teach a student the basics—to get him or her through elementary or high school with a minimum of grief. Others focus on preparing learning-disabled students for college or a career or enabling them to become a full member of society. The following is a sampling of programs for the learning disabled. Information about other programs is available through any of the organizations listed in the back of this book.

Landmark

Landmark, the largest school in the country for dyslexic students, is a residential, ungraded school for both elementary and secondary students in Prides Crossing, Massachusetts. Its high-school curriculum emphasizes remedial language skills as well as a full range of academic subjects. The staff–pupil ratio for most classes is one to three, though in the daily language tutorial the ratio is one to one. The school does not claim to cure dyslexia, although through a combination of drill, attention to detail, and strict discipline, its students often show a marked improvement.

Charles Drake, the school's founder (he is himself dyslexic), believes that one of Landmark's most important tasks is to bolster the self-confidence of its students. With this in mind, Drake began a sailing program called Watermark. Watermark students drawn from the Landmark student body spend a full year living and traveling on a large sailing ship, learning seamanship, marine science, history, and language skills and developing confidence and maturity along the way. As word of Landmark's success has spread, similar programs have developed, including a transitional college preparatory school, a two-year college in Putney, Vermont, and a branch campus for the learning disabled in California. Tuition for Landmark is high, but because all of Landmark's students qualify as handicapped under Federal Law 94–142, tuition payments are tax deductible.

Curry College

Unlike Landmark's students, most of Curry College's 1,200 students are not learning disabled. Indeed, Curry, which is located in Milton, Massachusetts, is a fully accredited four-year liberal arts college. However, in 1970, education specialist Dr. Gertrude Webb realized that Curry needed a special program for students capable of doing college work but lacking the necessary language and study skills. Dr. Webb was especially interested in students with active, creative minds who had difficulty with verbal expression or spatial perception. Her solution was PAL, a one-year

(continued on page 74)

One Student's Triumph

The following letter was written by a learning-disabled fourth grade student from the Landmark School in Prides Crossing, Massachusetts. The letter chronicles this student's frustrations, depression, and triumphs, ending with his feelings about his school. This letter is just one example of what a good learning-disability program can give back to an LD student: self-esteem and confidence.

Dyslexia   3/2/88

It was bad for me in catholic school. I was in first grade! Kid that I was stopit. I left school for reading I come back and forth, every day. It was not good at all. It help a little. I came out after school and I came in cry. Because kid said I was stopit and call my name. I did not have any freind. But my brother. I was not shor about him to. Then my brother fond out that I was spechel. Then I had more and more freinds. It was hard! Alway I wanted to kill my self. But 3 year agg it chang I came to Landmark. I did not want to kill my self. It has help me alot.

Dr. Gertrude Webb, director of PAL (Program for Advancement of Learning) at Curry College.

(continued from page 72)

program for advancement of learning. Most PAL students spend an intensive three weeks in July—before their freshman year begins—learning language and study skills and developing self-awareness. During their freshman year, PAL students carry a full academic load but also receive tutorial assistance from the college's learning center. The Curry faculty allows PAL students maximum flexibility so that they can take untimed tests, read with the assistance of audiotapes, and work on special alternative assignments. Dr. Webb emphasizes that the key to success for PAL students is knowing their personal learning strengths and developing a strong sense of self-worth.

Adelphi University

Located in Long Island, New York, Adelphi University has had a program for learning-disabled students since 1979. The program stresses academic and social adjustment. Adelphi helps its students cope with the problems and social stress of adapting to college life and interacting with other students.

The Gow School

Founded in 1926, the Gow School is the nation's oldest school for dyslexic students. Located in South Wales, a small town 30 miles southwest of Buffalo, New York, the Gow School—under headmaster David Gow (son of the founder)—offers a private boarding-school atmosphere to dyslexic young men who wish to prepare for college. The Gow School accepts students from 7th to 12th grades and puts them through a very thorough program. The boys' day begins at 6:45 A.M. and ends with lights out at 10:00 P.M., with a series of small classes, study periods, and athletics in between.

Students are required to take a reconstructive language course six days a week that drills them in the basics of speech and the written language. Tuition at the Gow School exceeds $9,000 a year, including room and board. According to a 1977 study done by researchers at the Johns Hopkins Medical School, a large majority of Gow graduates go on to receive a bachelor's degree in college. Half of these go on to hold jobs at the managerial level; others enter a technical or professional field; 10% receive advanced degrees.

STILE

Success Through Independent Living Experience (STILE) is a program based in Asbury Park, New Jersey, in which learning-disabled adults who range in age from 18 to 26 share a garden apartment house. Each resident receives food money each week and is responsible for the care and upkeep of his or her shared apartment as well as for a task assigned to the apartment house (e.g., sweeping the halls). Residents can stay with the program for three years, during which time they must hold down a job in the community.

At STILE, learning-disabled adults are taught economic skills, such as balancing a budget and paying bills, and are also schooled in social skills. Some learning-disabled persons have trouble acting appropriately in certain social situations. They may, for example, give vent to extreme emotions that puzzle or alarm other people. At STILE and in programs similar to it, these adults are

(continued on page 78)

The Gow School

In 1926 Peter Gow founded a school to educate young boys of at least average intelligence who were experiencing scholastic difficulties. The Gow School would become the first institute for dyslexics and is the oldest school of its kind in the world.

Located in the rural town of South Wales, 30 miles southwest of Buffalo, New York, the Gow School puts its 150 students through a rigorous college preparatory program. Whereas dyslexic students may have difficulty pursuing an education after high school, a study conducted by Johns Hopkins University indicates that 95% of students who graduate from the Gow School go on to college.

The school accepts students in grades 7–12. Although the student body is currently all male, head-

Headmaster David Gow, son of the late founder, Peter Gow, works with some students.

A Gow School basketball coach outlines a play.

master David Gow predicts that girls will be accepted in the not-too-distant future. The core of the Gow curriculum is a course in reconstructive language that focuses on phonetics, enabling the students to strengthen their basic language skills. After they master these skills, students can apply them in more advanced course work such as foreign languages.

Computers allow students to take advantage of different learning programs and tools. One such program is the spelling check program, particularly useful at Gow because most dyslexics are poor spellers as a consequence of their disorder. Another feature of the Gow School is the small size of its classes. Each class has only four or five students, so that each pupil can receive the special attention he needs to learn certain skills.

Gow students live at the school, which resembles a small college campus complete with dorms, cafeteria, infirmary, and library. Although time at Gow is strictly structured (the students' day begins at 7:00 A.M. and ends with lights out at 10:00 P.M.), the small the student body and the variety of extracurricular activities and programs at the school make it possible for the students to remain active and form close friendships. There are a number of sports programs available to students, and nearby skiing offers them additional opportunities for social contact.

The all-dyslexic student body is an appealing aspect of the Gow School. According to a 1984 article in the *New York Times Magazine*, most students at Gow find that being in the company of fellow dyslexics reduces the feeling of isolation that many of them often feel around non-learning-disabled students.

Students may remain at Gow for the full term (7th–12th grade) or attend for just a year or two. The school also accepts students who wish to complete a post–high school year of education before going on to college. Regardless of when they arrive, 85% of Gow students who are eligible to return after their first year do so.

(continued from page 75)

taught to recognize social signals and to tailor their behavior and emotions so that they suit given situations. After leaving STILE, the learning disabled are prepared to live independently, often choosing to do so within easy reach of the program and its directors. If a former resident chooses to remain nearby, all the resources of the program remain available to him or her.

There are a number of independent living programs like STILE throughout the country, including the following:

- Jewish Special Young Adults (JESPY), located in South Orange, New Jersey. In JESPY, learning-disabled Jewish adults age 18–30 live in apartments with 2 or more other residents and follow a program similar to that of STILE. A main goal of JESPY, however, is fostering a feeling of Jewish identity that may, in turn, bolster the residents' self-confidence and sense of belonging.

- Terry's Residence for Young Adults (TRYA), a program for learning-disabled young adults, located in Hempstead, New York. TYRA is funded by the state and private concerns; residents contribute half their tuition from social security checks or salary.

Other Alternatives

Although the right school or program can help the learning disabled greatly, individual or family psychotherapy is sometimes an essential adjunct to their treatment. Psychotherapy can help repair self-esteem and can identify family tensions that make learning difficult. Even mild depression about a learning problem can be reason enough to seek therapy. Many young people have so many learning deficits that the odds seem stacked against them. At times, a sensitive psychotherapist can help even the odds and, perhaps, offer a sympathetic ear to students who wish to discuss personal or family problems. Psychotherapy is often provided by schools or covered by comprehensive health insurance and thus can be fairly inexpensive.

• • • •

CHAPTER 8
. . . .
THE FUTURE IS BRIGHT

Much remains misunderstood about learning disabilities. There are still children, teenagers, and adults who suffer in silence. However, as we move into an era of increasingly sophisticated technology and public awareness, there may be fewer children who must endure the taunts of their classmates and more people who understand what is meant by the term *learning disabled*.

As research continues, progress in the field of learning disabilities is bound to continue. What do scientists hope to find in the future? First, geneticists hope for more information explaining the link between some learning problems—specifically dyslexia—and heredity. Once researchers identify the chromosome probably associated with reading problems, they may be able to predict at birth which children will have dyslexia.

What do educators hope to find in the future? Elementary-school teachers and parents will be more on the lookout for indications that children have learning problems. Teachers already seem eager for training in the area of learning differences and for instruction in new teaching methods. They also need to teach smaller classes. High school teachers hope that learning-disabled students will learn to speak up and ask for help. Many educators hope there will be less pressure on kindergarten children to begin reading. They hope more and more alternative programs will develop for disabled students on the high school and college level.

WHAT DO STUDENTS HOPE FOR?

Many students hope for the same developments anticipated by educators: better diagnosis, more help, smaller classes, alternative programs. Students want to feel capable and to see progress in their learning. They want to be judged on the basis of who they are and not what their handwriting or spelling looks like.

More immediately, many students long to get through school as best they can. They know there are many occupations in which a learning disability is not a grave handicap. In fact, most occupations are less stressful and more rewarding for the learning disabled than that of being a student. Many successful professionals cope with reading, writing, and numbers problems by dictating memos, color coding their files, developing compensating strengths, and working hard. However, most strategies available in the working world mask or circumvent learning problems rather than address them.

Learning specialists are less preoccupied with speculating about the future than with issues currently facing the field of learning-disability education. One issue is the cost of special education. Some school administrators argue that escalating special-education costs have reduced other school services. They say it is not fair for 35% of the education budget to be spent on only 10% of the students. Others debate the issue of who should pay for special education. How much of a burden should be shouldered by parents? By the community? By the federal government?

Other issues concern the schools' responsibility for educating learning-disabled young people. In 1984, a New Hampshire high school graduated a severely dyslexic girl who had not yet learned to read. The girl's parents demanded that school officials finance special post–high school education for their daughter, arguing that the school had neglected its responsibility to teach her to read. In another case, a journalism student filed a class-action suit against her college, demanding that the college waive its foreign-language requirement. She explained that for herself and other dyslexics learning a foreign language is impossibly difficult.

A teacher at the Gow School helps students work with a microscope. Many teachers hope that the future will bring smaller classes, enabling them to focus on the needs of a few students.

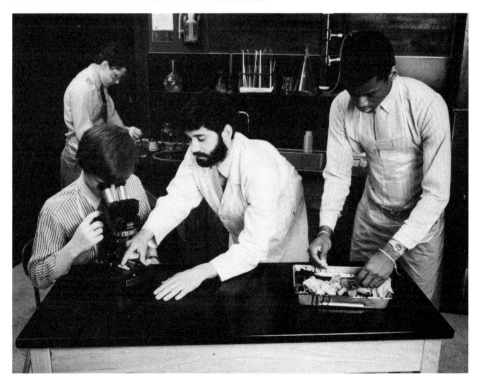

These cases raise serious questions. How far must everyone go in remedying learning problems? How accommodating should our schools be?

Still another issue involves the increasing numbers of students with learning problems. Are some of these problems being diagnosed incorrectly, or is the diagnostic procedure getting better? Is there something intrinsically wrong with an educational system that causes problems for so many young people? Are classroom teachers neglecting their responsibility to these students by assigning them to learning centers, or are teachers assigned so many students that they cannot give adequate attention to individual problems? Are normal learning differences being camouflaged as disabilities? These questions may never be answered to everyone's satisfaction.

We all look different on the outside. It is no surprise that our brains and personalities are different on the inside. Some people are gifted writers with unusually strong language ability. Some of us have severe language deficits. Some children have great natural ability for sports, whereas others panic when a ball is thrown to them. Some people believe in themselves and work hard. Others always seem depressed and ready to give up.

There are no easy solutions to learning disabilities—no answers written in stone. New technology, however, has provided more than one clue to the great mystery of the mind, the place where all answers to these questions and many others are hidden. While these answers are being sought, we can at least learn to cope with what we cannot yet cure. There are no miracle cures for learning disabilities, but with new technology and improved learning programs there is hope for a brighter future.

•   •   •   •

APPENDIX:
FOR MORE INFORMATION

The following is a list of associations and organizations that can provide information on learning disabilities and facilities and programs that treat the learning disabled.

ALABAMA

Montgomery Dyslexia Foundation
2229 Allendale Road
Montgomery, AL 36111
(205) 265-2840

ALASKA

Alaska Treatment Center
3710 East 20th Avenue
Anchorage, AK 99508
(907) 272-3720

ARIZONA

Center for Neurodevelopmental
   Studies, Inc.
8434 North 39th Avenue
Phoenix, AZ 85051
(602) 934-7166

ARKANSAS

Learning Center, College of the
   Ozarks
415 College Avenue
Clarksville, AR 72830
(501) 754-3839, ext. 421

LEARNING DISABILITIES

CALIFORNIA

CHILD, Clearing House for
Information on Learning
Disabilities
12327 Santa Monica Boulevard,
Suite 202
Los Angeles, CA 90025
(213) 207-8303

ERAS Center (Educational
Resource and Services Center)
9261 West Third Street
Beverly Hills, CA 90210
(213) 859-9731

COLORADO

Denver Academy
1101 South Race
Denver, CO 80210
(303) 777-5870

CONNECTICUT

Lake Grove at Durham
Wallingford Road
P.O. Box 659
Durham, CT 06422
(203) 349-3467

DELAWARE

The Pilot School, Inc.
100 Garden of Eden Road
Wilmington, DE 19803
(302) 478-1740

DISTRICT OF COLUMBIA

Lab School of Washington
4759 Reservoir Road NW
Washington, DC 20016
(202) 965-6600

FLORIDA

Developmental Center
105 5th Avenue NE
St. Petersburg, FL 33701
(813) 822-6914

GEORGIA

Reading Success, Inc.
3152 Washington Road, Suite 101
Augusta, GA 30907
(404) 255-5951

HAWAII

Fairhaven School
2062 South King Street
Honolulu, HI 96826
(808) 944-0173

ILLINOIS

Lawrence Hall School for Boys
4833 North Francisco
Chicago, IL 60625
(312) 769-3500

IOWA

Educational Resource Associates,
Inc.
8614 Harbach
Des Moines, IA 50322
(515) 225-8513

KANSAS

Diagnostic and Learning Center,
    Inc.
502 Wild Turkey
Emporia, KS 66801
(316) 342-7757

KENTUCKY

Meredith-Dunn Learning Center
3023 Melbourne Avenue
Louisville, KY 40220
(502) 895-3952

LOUISIANA

dePaul Dyslexia Association
9150 Bereford Drive
Baton Rouge, LA 70815
(504) 923-2068

MARYLAND

Center for Unique Learners
1220 Wilkins Avenue
Rockville, MD 20852
(301) 231-0115

MASSACHUSETTS

Community Providers of Adolescent
    Services, Inc. (COMPASS)
115 Warren Street
Roxbury, MA 02119
(617) 442-2181

MICHIGAN

Michigan Dyslexia Institute
4295 Okemos Road, Suite 1
Okemos, MI 48864
(517) 349-6522

MINNESOTA

Learning Disabilities Association
2344 Nicollet Avenue, Suite 200
Minneapolis, MN 55404
(612) 645-8124

MISSISSIPPI

Heritage School
Box 20434
301 Claiborne Avenue
Jackson, MS 39209
(601) 969-0603

MISSOURI

Edgewood Children's Center
330 North Gore
St. Louis, MO 63119
(314) 968-8936

NEBRASKA

Epworth Village, Inc./H. K.
    Daugherty Learning Center
Box 503
2100 Division Avenue
York, NE 68467
(402) 362-3353

NEVADA

Optimal-Ed Learning Center
1516 East Tropicana Avenue
Las Vegas, NV 89119
(702) 736-0706

NEW HAMPSHIRE

New England Speech Services
11 Chestnut Street
Dover, NH 03820
(603) 749-2446

NEW JERSEY

The Bancroft School
Hopkins Lane
Haddonfield, NJ 08033
(609) 429-0010

NEW MEXICO

Brush Ranch School, Inc.
P.O. Box 2450
Santa Fe, NM 87504-2450
(505) 757-6114

NEW YORK

Churchill School and Center for
   Learning Disabilities
2 East 95th Street
New York, NY 10128
(212) 722-0610

The Norman Howard School
220 Helendale Road
Rochester, NY 14609
(716) 288-3080

NORTH CAROLINA

Hill Learning Development Center
   of Durham Academy
3130 Pickett Road
Durham, NC 27705
(919) 489-7464

OHIO

Cincinnati Center for
   Developmental Disorders
3300 Elland Avenue
Cincinnati, OH 45229
(513) 559-4321

OKLAHOMA

Town and Country School
2931 East 31st Street
Tulsa, OK 74105
(918) 747-3679

OREGON

Mount Olive School for Dyslexic
   Children
1500 SW Greentree Avenue
Lake Oswego, OR 97034
(503) 636-1469

PENNSYLVANIA

Learning Disabilities Consultants
1021 Lancaster Avenue, Suite 205
Bryn Mawr, PA 19010
(215) 525-8336

RHODE ISLAND

Sargent Rehabilitation Center
229 Waterman Street
Providence, RI 02906
(401) 751-3113

SOUTH CAROLINA

Reading Success, Inc.
707 West Avenue
North Augusta, SC 29841
(803) 279-4503

TENNESSEE

Parent-Child Center of Knoxville
1016 Weisgarber Road, Suite 109
Knoxville, TN 37909
(615) 584-5558

TEXAS

Diagnostic and Remedial Reading
  Clinic
7310 Blanco Road, Suite 110
San Antonio, TX 78216
(512) 341-7417

UTAH

Specialized Educational
  Programming Service
1595 South 2100 East
Salt Lake City, UT 84108
(801) 582-7307

VERMONT

Center for Language and Learning
81 West Canal Street
Winooski, VT 05404
(802) 655-2332

VIRGINIA

D.T.C. Services (Diagnosing,
  Tutoring, Counseling of Learning
  Disabilities)
420 West Bute Street
Norfolk, VA 23510
(804) 625-6575

WASHINGTON

Co-operative Counseling Services
31003 "B" 18th Avenue South
Federal Way, WA 98003
(206) 941-2015

QUEBEC

Quebec Association for Children &
  Adults with Learning Disabilities
1181 Mountain Street
Montreal, Quebec H3G 1Z2
Canada
(514) 861-5518

LEARNING DISABILITIES

The following are some allied organizations and agencies serving learning disabled children and adults and their families.

Association for Children and Adults
  with Learning Disabilities
4156 Library Road
Pittsburgh, PA 15234
(412) 341-1515

National Center for Learning Disabilities
99 Park Avenue
New York, NY 10016
(212) 687-7211

National Association of Private
  Schools for Exceptional Children
2021 K Street NW
Washington, DC 20006
(202) 296-1800

The Orton Dyslexia Society
724 York Road
Baltimore, MD 21204
(301) 296-0232

FURTHER READING

Bettelheim, Bruno. *A Good Enough Parent*. New York: Knopf, 1987.

Bettelheim, Bruno, and Karen Zelan. *On Learning to Read*. New York: Knopf, 1982.

Blakeslee, Sandra. "Brain Studies Shed Light on Disorders." *New York Times*, November 11, 1984.

Bley, Nancy S. *Teaching Mathematics to the Learning Disabled*. Rockville, MD: Aspen Systems Corp., 1981.

Coles, Gerald. *The Learning Mystique*. New York: Pantheon Books, 1987.

Crow, Gary A. *Children at Risk*. New York: Schocken Books, 1978.

Cutter, Barbara C. *Unraveling the Special Education Maze*. Champaign, IL: Research Press, 1981.

Farnham-Diggory, Silvia. *Learning Disabilities*. Cambridge: Harvard University Press, 1978.

Flesh, Rudolf. *Why Johnny Still Can't Read*. New York: Harper & Row, 1981.

Gazzaniga, Michael S. *Mind Matters*. Boston: Houghton Mifflin, 1988.

Greene, Laurence J. *Kids Who Hate School: A Survival Handbook on Learning Disabilities*. Atlanta, GA: Humanics, Ltd., 1984.

Lamm, Stanley S. *Learning Disabilities Explained*. New York: Doubleday, 1982.

Lyman, Donald E. *Making the Words Stand Still.* Boston: Houghton Mifflin, 1986.

MacCracken, Mary. *Turnabout Children.* Boston: Little, Brown, 1986.

McGuiness, Diane. *When Children Don't Learn.* New York: Basic Books, 1985.

Moore, Raymond S., and Dorothy N. Moore. *Better Late Than Early.* New York: Reader's Digest Press, 1977.

Myers, Patricia I. *Learning Disabilities.* Austin, TX: Pro-Ed, 1982.

Osman, Betty B. *Learning Disabilities, A Family Affair.* New York: Warner Books, 1979.

Pernecke, Raegene B. *Schooling for the Learning Disabled: A Selective Guide to LD Programs in Elementary and Secondary Schools Throughout the U.S.* IL: SMS Publishers, 1983.

Robertson, Nan. "Where Learning-disabled Adults Learn to Cope." *New York Times*, June 10, 1980.

Rubin, Nancy. "State Programs Are Many and Varied." *New York Times*, November 11, 1984.

Scalfani, Annette Joy. *College Guide for Students with Learning Disabilities.* New York: Spedco Assoc., Inc., 1986.

Shore, Kenneth. *The Special Education Handbook.* New York: Warner Books, 1986.

Simmons, Nicole. "How L.D.'s Are Handled in New York's Schools." *New York Times*, November 11, 1984.

Springer, Sally P., and George Deutsch. *Left Brain, Right Brain.* San Francisco: W. H. Freeman and Co., 1981.

Sullivan, Margaret. "First School for Dyslexia Began in 20's." *New York Times*, November 11, 1984.

Vail, Priscilla L. *Smart Kids with School Problems*. New York: Dutton, 1987.

Vitale, Barbara Meister. *Unicorns Are Real: A Right-brained Approach to Learning*. Rolling Hills Estates, CA: Jalmar Press, 1982.

Weinstein, Bob. "Many Colleges Now Offer L.D. Programs." *New York Times*, November 11, 1984.

Williams, Linda V. *Teaching for the Two-sided Mind*. Englewood Cliffs, NJ: Prentice-Hall, 1983.

Winslow, Ron. "College for the Learning Disabled." *New York Times Magazine*, February 21, 1982.

GLOSSARY

ADHD attention deficit hyperactive disorder; a disorder that inhibits those afflicted with it from focusing on a single task, concentrating for an extended period of time, or screening out distracting information

corpus callosum the collective nerve fibers that connect the left and right hemispheres of the brain and that are more numerous and disorganized in dyslexics than in most people

dyscalculia a term that refers to difficulties some people have recognizing numbers and understanding basic mathematical concepts

dyslexia a term used to describe learning disorders involving written or spoken language and characterized by extreme difficulty learning and remembering letters, written or spoken words, and individual letter sounds

genetic inherited

hyperactivity a disorder in which a child cannot willingly control his or her "wild" behavior and may fluctuate from moments of quiet and industriousness to moments when he or she is noisy and disruptive

IEP individualized educational program; a special educational plan required by law for qualified learning disabled students that assesses a student's current strengths and weaknesses and outlines his or her reasonable short-term objectives and long-term goals

learning disability any of a wide range of disorders affecting people of at least normal intelligence, most of which impair reading or mathematical skills, but which may also affect writing, listening, speaking, and reasoning abilities

left hemisphere the side of the brain that contains areas specialized in the production and comprehension of language and is associated with orderly, precise thinking

mainstreaming a method by which learning-disabled children are given additional support in the form of a special class or tutorial but are able to attend and participate in regular classes

neurotransmitters chemicals that transmit nerve impulses across synapses

right hemisphere the half of the brain that contains areas specialized in visual perception, music, and emotions and is associated with instinctive and nonverbal responses

Ritalin the brand name for the stimulant drug methylphenidate, which may effect a positive physiological response in some ADHD patients

spatial deficit disorder in which an individual has difficulty judging his or her own body in relation to space and consequently seems clumsy and accident prone; this problem may include poor muscle coordination and balance

WISC-R the Wechsler Intelligence Scale for Children-Revised; the most widely used diagnostic test for children ages 6–16

word blindness a learning disorder in which the individual is able to discern individual letters but cannot recognize entire words

INDEX

PICTURE CREDITS

Susan Berkowitz/Taurus Photos: pp. 28, 50; Marion Bernstein/Art Resource: p. 37; The Bettmann Archive: p. 19; Courtesy of Bruce Byers/The Gow School: pp. 61, 76, 77, 81; Paul Conklin/Monkmeyer Press: p. 22; Laimute Druskis/Taurus Photos: pp. 21, 51, 53; Mimi Forsyth/Monkmeyer Press: pp. 15, 55; Courtesy of Albert M. Galaburda/Harvard Medical School: p. 47; Elizabeth Glasgow/Monkmeyer Press: p. 55; Debra P. Hershkowitz: pp. 31, 57; Bradford F. Herzog/Curry College: p. 74; Courtesy of Landmark: pp. 63, 67, 71, 73, 79; Edward Lettau/FPG International: cover; Courtesy of William Mills/Montgomery County Public Schools: p. 26; Cliff Moore/Taurus Photos: p. 13; Courtesy of the National Institute of Neurological and Communicative Disorders and Stroke: p. 41; Courtesy of the Orton Dyslexia Society: p. 17; Christy Park/Monkmeyer Press: p. 33; Karen Preuss/Taurus Photos: p. 65; Nisa Rauschenberg: pp. 43, 46; Shirley Zeiberg/Taurus Photos: p. 79

Jean McBee Knox is a writer who specializes in medicine and social issues. She is the author of *Drugs Through the Ages* for Chelsea House's ENCYCLO-PEDIA OF PSYCHOACTIVE DRUGS SERIES 2, and *Death and Dying* for Chelsea House's ENCYCLOPEDIA OF HEALTH. Her articles have appeared in the *Boston Globe*, the *Globe Sunday Magazine*, the *Christian Monitor*, and other publications. A graduate of Wheaton College and Wesleyan University, she has taught English in Greenwich, Connecticut, and Winchester, Massachusetts.

Solomon H. Snyder, M.D., is Distinguished Service Professor of Neuroscience, Pharmacology, and Psychiatry and director of the Department of Neuroscience at the Johns Hopkins University School of Medicine. He has served as president of the Society for Neuroscience and in 1978 received the Albert Lasker Award in Medical Research for his discovery of opiate receptors in the brain. Dr. Snyder is a member of the National Academy of Sciences and a Fellow of the American Academy of Arts and Sciences. He is the author of *Drugs and the Brain, Uses of Marijuana, Madness and the Brain, The Troubled Mind*, and *Biological Aspects of Mental Disorder*. He is also the general editor of Chelsea House's ENCYCLOPEDIA OF PSYCHOACTIVE DRUGS.

C. Everett Koop, M.D., Sc.D., is Surgeon General, Deputy Assistant Secretary for Health, and Director of the Office of International Health of the U.S. Public Health Service. A pediatric surgeon with an international reputation, he was previously surgeon-in-chief of Children's Hospital of Philadelphia and professor of pediatric surgery and pediatrics at the University of Pennsylvania. Dr. Koop is the author of more than 175 articles and books on the practice of medicine. He has served as surgery editor of the *Journal of Clinical Pediatrics* and editor-in-chief of the *Journal of Pediatric Surgery*. Dr. Koop has received nine honorary degrees and numerous other awards, including the Denis Brown Gold Medal of the British Association of Paediatric Surgeons, the William E. Ladd Gold Medal of the American Academy of Pediatrics, and the Copernicus Medal of the Surgical Society of Poland. He is a Chevalier of the French Legion of Honor and a member of the Royal College of Surgeons, London.